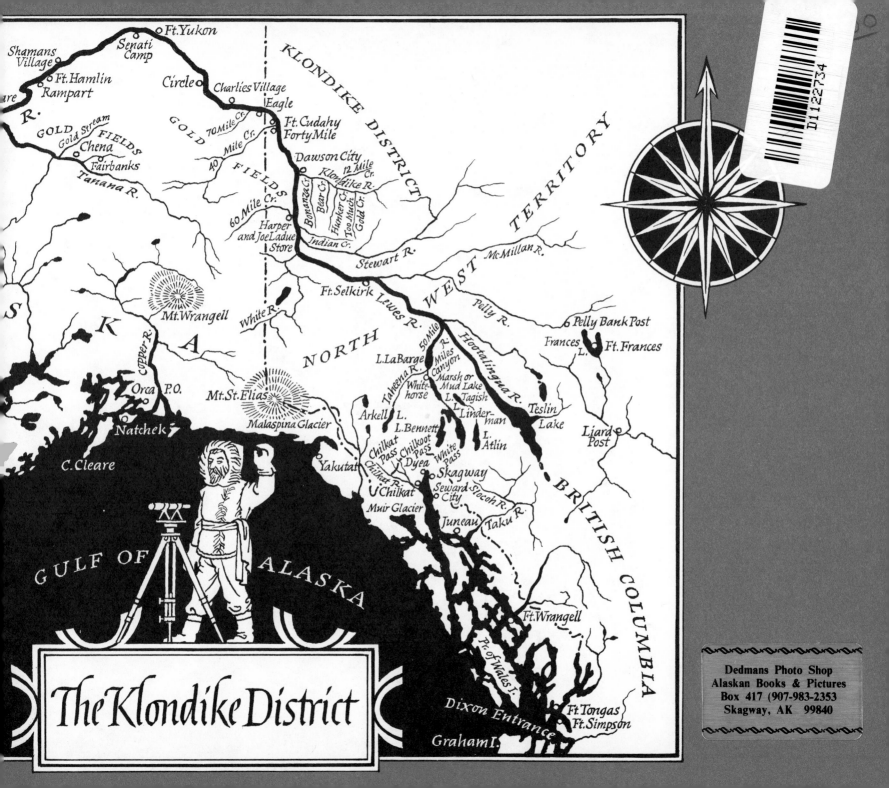

The Klondike District

ONE MAN'S GOLD RUSH

A Klondike Album

BY MURRAY MORGAN

Photographs by E. A. Hegg

University of Washington Press
SEATTLE AND LONDON
Douglas & McIntyre
VANCOUVER

Photograph on page 88 courtesy of the Library of Congress

This book is for JIM and ANN

Contents

Maps

ONE MAN'S GOLD RUSH

A Klondike Album

The Making of a Klondiker

E. A. HEGG was a man of few words but many pictures. This is our good fortune. His prose can most kindly be described as serviceable, but the best of his photographs approach greatness. Most of Hegg's letters and photographic plates disappeared during his lifetime, but many of the plates—far more numerous than the writings—have been recovered.

If we had to choose between Hegg's written observations about Alaska and the Yukon during the gold rushes and his photographs of the same events, the choice would surely be what chance, and the efforts of dedicated collectors, especially Ethel Anderson Becker, have returned to us. Still, it would be interesting to know more about the personal adventures and photographic techniques of Hegg than we do.

He was one of that breed of peripatetic artisans who opened studios across the continent in the period between the Civil and Spanish-American wars. A journeyman, largely self-trained, Hegg showed competence but not brilliance in his early work. Had he not joined the stampede to the Yukon, he probably would be remembered today only by the grandchildren and great-grandchildren of early settlers as they thumb family albums.

But Hegg did rush north with the Klondikers in 1897. He forced a sled load of photographic equipment across the coastal mountains in the dead of winter. He shot the rapids of the Yukon on the spring thaw. He hiked out to the claims on Bonanza and Eldorado, and he poked his camera into the banks and bars and bordellos in Dawson. He rode a paddle-wheel steamer down the Yukon to the Bering and was on the dark sands of the beach at Nome when the prospectors swirled gravel in their pans and worked their mechanical rockers. He stayed in the North to photograph the industrialization of gold mining as huge dredges were brought in to sluice out pay dirt from the treeless hills. He traveled with Eskimo sealers and railroad surveyors. But most important, he was there, high on the Chilkoot Pass in the winter of 1897-98, as the dark-clad men climbed antlike up the frozen steps of The Scales under the burden of a year's supplies. He photographed a migration unique in human history.

Shooting between snow squalls in temperatures that fell to minus thirty, working with a bulky camera and wet glass plates that had to be sensitized with chemicals every morning that offered the hint of enough sun to make photography possible, forced to improvise with herbs and the albumen of eggs when materials ran short (the nearest chemical shop was six hundred miles to the south), wetting his papers and developing his plates in a makeshift tent darkroom heated by a stove for which he man-hauled wood up the mountainside, Hegg achieved photographs that, better than any other individual record, reflect the folly and glory of the stampede to the Klondike.

When struck by Klondike fever, Eric Hegg was twenty-nine years old, a modestly successful man, the proprietor of two small photographic studios in neighboring hamlets on Bellingham Bay. Born in Bollnäs, inland from the eastern coast of Sweden, north of Stockholm, in 1868, he was brought to America by his parents when he was three. The Hegg family settled in Wisconsin. Eric attended grade school, then studied art and photography, presumably as apprentice to some local practitioner. Aged fifteen, he opened his own studio in Washburn, Wisconsin.

The year he turned twenty-one, Hegg was lured to the Puget Sound country, probably by the promotion efforts of the Northern Pacific, which had completed its tunnel through the Cascade Mountains and was promoting its company-owned townsite at Tacoma, "where the steel of rail meets the salt of ocean water," as the destined metropolis of the Far West. It was at the clapboard depot at Seventeenth and Commerce in Tacoma that Hegg unloaded his camera and chemicals late in the summer of 1888.

Tacoma was smitten by what a visiting British reporter, Rudyard Kipling, called "a boom of the boomiest." The town already boasted a generous supply of photographers. Three studios were operating within a hundred yards of the main intersection, and the narrow store buildings along the boardwalks commanded rents of 150 dollars a month or more. Hegg decided Tacoma was too mature to be the place for him to settle and grow up with the country.

Nelson Bennett, the big, black-bearded contractor who had rammed the rails through the Stampede Pass for the Northern Pacific, was investing some of his earnings in a new townsite on Bellingham Bay. To connect his new community with the ports of southern Puget Sound, Bennett had a 130-foot stern-wheeler built at the Holland shipyard in Tacoma. He named the vessel *Fairhaven* after his proposed town, and on her first trip north sold tickets one way to Bellingham Bay for a dollar, the round trip costing seven. Hegg took advantage of the bargain rate north and stayed in the Bellingham area for nearly ten years.

He opened his first studio in Sehome, also known as New Whatcom; it stood on what is now the site of the Alaska Building in Bellingham. A year or two later he set up a second studio in Fairhaven, which had developed into a lively community dedicated to logging, mining, and entertaining lonely miners and loggers.

The few of Hegg's pictures that survive from his stay on Bellingham Bay indicate that although photographing weddings and christenings may have been his means of paying bills, he preferred to work out of doors. His greatest interest lay in recording scenes that showed men in contest with nature.

Commercial fishing was then becoming an important industry on Puget Sound. Hegg took pictures of the Lummi Indians as they went out in their dark dugouts to place nets that would intercept the annual runs of sockeye salmon

headed north for their spawning beds on the Fraser River. And he took some of the first photographs of the commercial fish traps the white fishermen were installing on the northern reaches of the Sound.

The commercial traps, a modification of the Indian method of harvesting the salmon runs, were the most efficient method of catching salmon ever devised. The trap consisted of wire netting fastened to log pilings driven for half a mile or more across a path salmon were known to follow on their return from the ocean to their native stream

to spawn. The wire net forced the fish to swim down a narrowing V, at the head of which was an opening to a second, smaller V, called the heart. This in turn ended in a pot—a wire enclosure that held the fish trapped. From the pot a control gate could be opened to allow the salmon to pass through a net tunnel in a spiller, where they were netted—"brailed"—and pulled into a scow for transportation to the cannery. Hegg's photos of the traps in operation document the industrialization of the Puget Sound salmon fishery.

The quiet young Swede also packed his camera and glass plates and chemicals back into the woods with the loggers of Bellingham Bay. Here too he recorded the mechanization of what had been a brute-power business. One of his best photographs catches the quiet charm of an overaged skid road—the path of notched logs down which ox teams hauled logs to the mills or to rafting areas at tidewater.

Deep in the woods Hegg found enough sunlight to preserve on film the pride of the fallers, those muscular timber beasts who drove narrow springboards into the conifers above the jungle undergrowth and, balanced on these perches, attacked the giant cedars and firs with double-bitted axes and two-man saws.

He focused, too, on the upright donkey-engines—"tin cans with anchors," some called them—that during the 1890's were replacing oxen as the instruments for yarding logs into central clearings; and on the tiny logging locomotives—"dinkeys"—that pulled the logs out of the forest over tracks that had no business staying together, and often didn't.

Unconsciously, Hegg was training himself to be a photographer of industry and the epic. He was ready when the call to adventure came.

The New Whatcom *Reveille* reported, during the third week of July, 1897, that two ships carrying gold had put into Pacific Coast ports.

The dirty, rusty, stubby *Excelsior*, operated by the Alaska Commercial Company, docked July 15 at San Francisco. She carried a score of prospectors and nearly a thousand pounds of gold. Among the passengers were Mr. and Mrs. Tom Lippy of Seattle. Now, Tom Lippy was somebody nearly everybody on Puget Sound knew or knew of—the 1890's equivalent of a high school coach. He had been a clerk and physical education instructor at the Seattle YMCA, a wiry little man whose notable attributes were niceness and physical coordination. He had tired of YMCA penury and taken a fling at prospecting, just another nice guy chasing rainbows before subsiding back into the everyday. But here was a story of Tom Lippy staggering down the gangplank of the *Excelsior*, barely able to manage, even with his wife's assistance, the burden of his suitcase. It held more than two hundred pounds in nuggets and gold dust. Gold then averaged seventeen dollars an ounce. You could pencil it out—seventeen dollars an ounce, sixteen ounces to a pound, two hundred pounds in the suitcase: why Good Old Tom was bringing out more than 54,400 dollars.

The *Excelsior's* arrival in San Francisco was unheralded. But the wires carried word north that a second and richer ship was due in Seattle. Five thousand persons were waiting at Schwabacher's dock when at six o'clock on the morning of July 17, the North American Trading and Transporting Company's *Portland*, larger, dirtier, and more gold encumbered, edged up to the wharf. Beriah Brown, an en-

terprising reporter for the Seattle *Post-Intelligencer*, had boarded her from a chartered boat as she entered the Strait of Juan de Fuca and, with echoing understatement, had telegraphed that she was carrying "more than a ton of solid gold." The fact is that the *Portland*, once reputed to be a jinx ship,* was bringing out about two tons.

* *She had once been seized by the Haitian government for carrying ammunition to rebels during a civil war, and had been condemned and seized by United States authorities after illegal Chinese immigrants and opium were found aboard her.*

Most important, the prospectors brought word that there was more gold, much more, where theirs had been found, on the Klondike, a tributary of the Yukon. Until then the name Klondike had been known to few, and to them it had connoted salmon rather than gold. The word, often spelled "Clondyke" in first reports, is thought to be a corruption of "Thron-diuck," an Indian word which translates as "hammer water" and is said to derive from the fact that the natives drove stakes across the shallow mouth of the stream as anchors for their salmon nets.

The name of the Klondike was not entirely unfamiliar to Hegg. Three months before the gold ships docked, A. H. Miller, who had run a restaurant and cigar store in New Whatcom, not far from Hegg's studio, came Outside from Alaska with a rumor of a big strike on the Klondike. Miller sought to raise money to start a hotel at the head of Lynn Canal, a natural waterway six hundred miles south of the Klondike but the nearest point to it on salt water. His stories of an impending rush excited some of Bellingham Bay's adventurous young men. A party of six persons well known to Hegg left on April Fool's Day, prepared they said to stay three years if that was what it took to find gold. (Most were back in six months, broke.) A second and larger expedition caught the May sailing of the side-wheeler *George E. Starr*. But Miller had brought out no gold, only rumors of gold, and prudent men discounted rumors.

It was a time when there was magic in the word "gold"—

but where there is magic, there is disbelief. The country lay bogged in the long depression that grew out of the panic of 1893. The Puget Sound building boom that had swelled out of the completion of the Northern Pacific's lines to tidewater had collapsed with an abruptness that ruined thousands. Workmen who had pushed steel over, and sometimes dangerously through, the mountains found themselves unemployed. They moved unwelcomed into the cities, where jobs were few. Farm prices collapsed. And while Nature's bounty prevented much actual starvation in the Pacific Northwest, there were few cash crops, and almost no cash. It was said that the exact location of every double-eagle gold piece in every town was known each night to all bankers and merchants. The shortage of gold was the curse of the common man, and William Jennings Bryan's call for inflation echoed loud in the land.

Thus, there was a fairy story quality to the reports of men, strong men, men whose names were familiar in the community and whose weaknesses were familiar in bar and barber shop, lurching ashore under the burden of wealth greater than a former neighbor should be called upon to carry alone. Every detail incited avarice. The golden nuggets, it was said, had jagged edges—evidence that they had not been washed far from the mother lode. Riches still greater awaited the enterprising.

On the strength of Beriah Brown's scoop for the *P-I* about her cargo, the *Portland* was booked full for her return voyage even before she reached Seattle. Among the fifty passengers going first cabin was John H. McGraw, immediate past governor of the state of Washington. If more surety were needed about the authenticity of hope, Colonel W. D. Wood, mayor of Seattle, who chanced to be in San Francisco when the *Excelsior* put in, had wired his resignation to the city council, to be accepted if he succeeded in organizing an expedition north and failed to return to Seattle before the council became restive or his statutory period of absences ran out.*

Within three hours of the docking of the *Portland*, Se-

Mayor Wood's resignation was accepted. His misadventures make up one of the bittersweet stories of the stampede. He chartered an old California riverboat, the Humboldt, *for the run to the mouth of the Yukon. So many Californians joined his expedition that it was impossible to load all their provisions. When the captain tried to depart without much of the gear, Wood barely escaped lynching. The* Humboldt *eventually reached St. Michael, a clapboard town squatting on the flats of the Yukon delta, and only then did the passengers find that they were expected to help build a new steamer for the voyage up the river. Not without complaint, they assembled a craft officially called* Seattle Number One, *but popularly known as the* Mukluk, *because of its resemblance to that soft, unshaped Eskimo footgear. The* Mukluk *failed to reach the Klondike before the Yukon froze, and Mayor Wood, who had laid in provender to sell the prospectors on the Klondike, was persuaded, not without threat of violence, to meet the needs of the ice-bound at Seattle prices. Everybody survived. When they reached Dawson City, 314 days out of San Francisco, nearly all tried immediately to book passage home. Not everyone made it back that year, but of those who had to stay behind, none struck it rich.*

attle's waterfront streets were so crowded that horse-drawn trams couldn't push through the press. Some teamsters simply dropped their reins and hustled to the booking office, where they found themselves competing for passage north with bank clerks, whistle punks, cooks and bull cooks, attorneys, pimps, fishermen, merchants, ministers, the more prescient of the box-house girls from the Skid Road, and even an occasional experienced prospector. Unions and congregations and social clubs were holding meetings to raise funds and send representatives north to stake claims. As the crowds pressed up to the ticket desk, newsboys hawked papers that detailed the good fortune of the sixty-eight sourdoughs who had just debarked:

Nils Anderson of Seattle, who had been unable to find work in the lumber camps in the summer of 1895, had borrowed three hundred dollars and gone north with nothing in his favor except desperation. His wife, whom he had left with several small children and no income, had heard he was on his way out and was waiting on the dock, hopeful that their luck had changed. Indeed it had. Anderson debarked with so much gold a friend had to help him carry it—112,500 dollars' worth.

Another Scandinavian rushed to the express office with a canvas sack he wanted to forward to the mint at San Francisco, Seattle having no assay office at the time. "I tank I have twenty tousand five huner dollar," he told the clerk, who put the gold on the scales and corrected him. It weighed out at approximately forty-two thousand dollars.

William Stanley of Anacortes had left his wife with only twenty dollars when he went north. She had been supporting herself by taking in washing and picking blackberries. She hadn't heard that he was coming Outside. He wired her from Seattle to stop washing and start buying, they were worth ninety thousand dollars.

So the stories went, losing little in the telling. The call of gold echoed across the country. It boomed loud and clear on Bellingham Bay. Eric Hegg was among the first to respond. He seems not to have thought of prospecting but only of photographing the rush. It was not gold but excitement —and a chance to practice his trade—that lured him. He locked the doors of his two studios, entrusted the keys to his younger brother Peter, who had followed him west from Wisconsin, bought all the chemicals and plates and paper he could afford, and went to Seattle to seek passage to the Yukon.

The Way North

TWO ROUTES led north.

The traditional way into the interior of Alaska and the Yukon Territory was the All Water Passage by way of the Pacific, the Bering, and the Yukon. It involved a round-about trip of 4,200 miles or more: from Seattle to the mouth of the Yukon, it was agreed, was about 2,800 miles, but every riverboat captain had his own guess about how far up the river Dawson lay. Some said 1,250 miles, others 2,250 miles, and 1,600 miles was the favorite estimate.

Under favorable circumstances the voyage took about forty days—but it might require eight months. The Yukon usually becomes navigable in May, but the Bering doesn't open as far as St. Michael until late June and freezes in late September. The danger of being caught aboard a river boat between St. Michael and the Klondike was considerable. Even so, there were more passengers than berths. The problem for those wanting to take the ocean and river route was finding passage.

The more direct but more difficult Water and Overland route was used by ten times as many Klondikers as went all the way by boat. The water portion of the shorter route followed the protected sea lanes between the rim of the continent and the fretwork of islands off the British Columbia and Alaska coasts. The islands screened the Inside Passage from the full force of the Pacific storms. Ships unfit for the unprotected water of the Gulf of Alaska and the Bering could be pressed into service between Puget Sound and the various northern termini that boasted of offering the easiest way through the mountains to the Yukon.

The established ports of embarkation—Seattle, Tacoma, Victoria, and Port Townsend, and to a lesser degree Portland and San Francisco—were confusions of activity as shipyards blossomed to build new craft and refurbish relics going back to the first days of steam on the Pacific Coast. Comfort was nothing and safety a minor consideration; capacity was all. Colliers were diverted from the coal trade, and their holds were converted into stables for the horses needed to pack food and prospecting gear across the mountains. Many ships sailed with bales of hay stacked on the bridge. Bunks were tacked everywhere. Tents were pitched in lifeboats. On most ships the only spot considered sacrosanct was the saloon.*

While the stampeders waited for their ships to be fitted, they explored such mysteries as that of the diamond hitch, said to be the only device for holding a load on a horse's back on the trails through the St. Elias Range, or they dickered with horse traders, whose asking price was twenty-five dollars for any brute still breathing.

"The horses that are being offered for packing over the hardest kind of trail!" a reporter exclaimed. "Such ambulating bone-yards, the infirm and decrepit, those afflicted with spavins, the spring-halt, some with ribs like the sides of a whiskey case and hips to hang hats on. With their drooping heads and listless tails they look as if a good feed of oats would either break their backs or make them sag beyond remedy."

---

* *Captain Arthur H. Lee, R. A., of the Royal Military College in Kingston, Ontario, reported the Rush for the London* Chronicle. *In a note to the editor of a New York magazine, he alleged that the magazine's writer-photographer "even shed his blood one night in your behalf. I think he wanted to convert the saloon into a photographic dark-room, and some inconsiderate gold-seeker objected with much and destructive violence. However, he was well and cheery the last I saw of him."*

For a time the streets were snarled with sled dogs, some real, mostly alleged, all carrying prices like ransoms. Then the available supply of dogs was exhausted. "Seattle," said a reporter for the *Argus*, "has become a cat's paradise."

When a ship did sail, horses whinnying in fright in their two-foot-wide stalls, prospectors (most of them still in dark business suits) lining the rail or sitting on the bales of hay, the docks black with well-wishers, there were cheers back and forth for the Klondike, cheers for gold. "God does not give us many scenes like this," said the poet Joachin Miller as he sailed aboard the *Mexico*, which, on her return voyage, speared herself while running full bore through the dangerous waters south of Sitka.

Other ships simply disappeared. Some jammed themselves aground in the fogs that formed as the warm wet winds from off the Japanese current cooled when rising over the islands. But the demand for passage north remained greater than the capacity of the vessels in service.

Eric Hegg roamed the waterfront looking for photographs and, more important, passage north. The photos came easy, and he got some good ones of crowded docks and of the waterfront stores spilling their wares across sidewalk and street. But passage was hard to find.

All ships scheduled for 1897 were booked beyond capacity before Hegg reached Seattle. As additional ships were diverted into service north, the price of tickets shot up. Some men settled for deck passage and no baggage in the expectation that they would be able to buy supplies in Alaska. But Hegg doubted that he would be able to acquire photographic supplies up there.

Eventually he joined a party of Bellingham Bay men in chartering the *Skagit Chief*, a small stern-wheeler that had been built in Tacoma in 1889 for service on the Sound and the lower reaches of the Skagit River but, a victim of the Depression and an enigmatic engine, was lying idle at New Whatcom. She was small for the run north, even by way of the Inside Passage, but she was available.

There are two versions of Hegg's voyage. One says that the Hegg party was able to get the *Skagit Chief* into working order and that she trailed a pair of barges behind her all the way to Dyea. The other has her towed north by a tug.

"How we ever made it still seems an act of Providence," Hegg told a reporter some forty years later. "Terrific storms caused the barge to break up and once the tow-line snapped."

The reference to storms indicates that Hegg's trip was made in late September or early October, when several severe gales struck the coast that year. But even with clouds stretching from the hilltops of the westward islands to the forested foothills to starboard, the Passage is entrancing: the forests almost unbroken, the water a heavy green, excited by an occasional school of porpoises or pod of killer whales; the mystery of the shoreline deepened by Indian villages at water's edge, with totem poles, grotesque and beautiful, facing the sea. Sometimes they saw Indian canoes, high prows exquisitely streamlined and barbarically decorated, hulls blackened with soot and seal oil.

"Crawling along under the somber shadows of the dense overhanging trees in the deep passages," one observer noted, "these canoes can hardly be seen until very near, and when a flash of water from the paddle reveals their presence they look more like smugglers or pirates avoiding notice than anything else."

There were few ports of call along the Passage, and those surpassing strange. Wrangell, "the most tumble-down looking company of cabins I ever saw," in the opinion of a laurente of the Paris Geographical Society, but prospering nonetheless on the sale of Indian trinkets, prospectors' supplies, and medicinal liquor, Alaska being in theory dry; Sitka—the former Russian capital, a town older than San Francisco and with a lovelier harbor; Juneau, already settled into its role of a no-nonsense industrial town of boardwalks and merchants who knew the advantage of having distance to blame prices on.

Hegg photographed them all. His best picture of the voyage north was of Indian boats drawn up on the bank of a river opening off the Lynn Canal, the natural waterway which runs to the foot of the mountains dividing the sea from the Yukon and the gold-rich interior. It is a great picture: the mystery of an alien way of life in the foreground, the challenge of the continent in the distance.

The *Skagit Chief* moved up the canal, the forests of cedar and spruce somber on mountains improbably near, glaciers pouring down valleys to plunge silently into the sea, the men aboard quiet with the realization of the adventure on which they had embarked.

The way north led through land-locked waters. Wrangell Narrows looked placid but was treacherous.

A French geographer described Wrangell, one of the first ports in Alaska, as "the most tumble-down looking company of cabins I ever saw."

Between the salt water and the forest were occasional stands of Indian totems and burial houses. These are at Hawkan.

Sitka, the old Russian capital, was the most cultured community in Alaska at the time of the gold rush. Baranof's Castle, as the former Russian administrative headquarters was called, stands on the hill at the right.

Juneau, the new capital, was the last supply port on the way to Skagway and Dyea.

Going up Lynn Canal: In the foreground, the mystery of an alien way of life, the challenge of the continent beyond.

Dyea and the Chilkoot Pass

THE *Skagit Chief* reached Dyea early in the fall of 1897. Ships anchored well offshore in the mountain-bound harbor. There is a twenty-foot spread between high and low tides, and the bore of the waters up the narrow inlet is swift and dangerous. It was up to the Klondikers to beach their gear. Passage did not include landing costs.

At Juneau, if not before, the men on the commercial passenger boats had been told of the landing problems ahead. On most ships the passengers elected a beach command party to supervise unloading. Lots were drawn on ship for precedence; cargo was put over the side in the order of the draw, unless general convenience dictated otherwise. No one was supposed to claim his goods on the beach until all the cargo was ashore, though most did, for to leave it untouched was to risk having it caught by the next high tide.

The ships carried rude scows of casual seaworthiness, which were used for lightering cargo, then were broken up and sold board by board to the lumber-hungry men ashore. Horses—most of them old and many already crippled—were swung over the side in slings and dropped into the bay to find their own way to the beach. Lumber was simply dumped over the side on an incoming tide; it was up to the owner to corral the boards and chivvy them ashore. When time was a factor, even the bales of hay were floated in.

Hegg's own problems in getting ashore are not on record.

But he photographed the difficulties faced by his peers. Gray, soggy, and dismal, the tidal beach stretched up to a dreary plain furrowed by the Dyea River and rutted by the wheels of wagons. The plain was piled with the impedimenta of the Klondikers, great stacks of food and blankets, stoves and sleds, boats of strange design and portable pianos, and casks that gurgled and were marked "medicine."

A quarter mile back from the beach wrack, the first tents blossomed. Another quarter mile and board buildings formed a funnel through which a muddy street led back toward the mountains. Thus Dyea.

A year earlier a visiting official described the place as "an Indian village of 250, a white town of four." The Indians were Chilkats, a member of the Tlingit family. They were a short, swart people, the men broad-shouldered and addicted to mustaches that were sparse though sweeping; the women equally broad-shouldered and given to blackening their faces with a mixture of grass and soot, for beauty's sake. Their habitations were small, crowded, and redolent of fish. The white man's town had consisted of a single frame building, used as both store and house.

Estimates of Dyea's population in the fall of 1897 range from three thousand to ten thousand. They probably would go higher had there been a Chamber of Commerce. The town offered clapboard hotels of minimal comfort, log cabin restaurants, tent saloons, open-air real estate dealers,

and other establishments where a man could dispose of money rapidly. Its reason for existence was a notch in the mountains, some twenty miles distant, which long had been the favorite path of Indians and experienced explorers going to and from the interior.

"A trail in Alaska," wrote one veteran of this route, "should not be confused with the ordinary highway of settled states. When a trail is spoken of as existing between two points in Alaska it has no further meaning than that a man, and possibly a beast of burden, may travel that way over the natural surface of the ground. There is a very strong improbability concerning the beast, unless it be a dog. The path may consist of nothing more than a marked or blazed way through an otherwise impenetrable wilderness, and unless it is used more or less continuously the traces are apt to disappear in one of Alaska's seasons. No eager prospector stops to make it easier for someone else. A man carrying his food, his cooking utensils, and working tools on his back has no time nor disposition to cut down trees. When he comes to an unfrozen stream he wades it, or if a tree has fallen across it so much the better. The Chilkoot trail possessed the advantage of having been used by miners since 1880 but it was laid out by Indians, who are too lazy to improve it; and besides, they make a living because it is almost impossible for pack animals to go over it."

At first the Chilkats monopolized the packing business out of Dyea. It was their pass, though storekeepers Healy and Wilson had improved the first few miles of the trail slightly and for a time were able to persuade the Klondikers to pay tolls.

The Chilkat bearers initially charged twelve cents a pound to carry goods the twenty-seven miles across the pass to the upper end of Lake Linderman. By the end of the first season of the rush the price had risen to thirty-eight cents a pound for goods in convenient packages, higher for lumber, stoves, pianos, trunks, and other oddly shaped impedimenta. They were physically powerful, the Chilkats, knowledgeable about the trail, shrewd and not unaware of the advantages of a monopoly to the monopolist. But what the Klondikers objected to most about the Indians was that they were Presbyterian, Christians to a fault: they wouldn't work on Sundays. Other days, however, they shrugged into harness, straightened under loads of up to two hundred pounds (women and children carried "a white man's burden"—seventy-five pounds), and shuffled up the trail, undeterred by anything except rumor that someone was receiving more pay per pound—information that usually precipitated a strike.

The Canadian authorities, fearful that more persons were getting into the territory than the wilderness could support, insisted that each man bring supplies for a year. That roughed out at a ton of goods per man. Few could afford to hire anyone to move such a quantity. It was do-it-yourself, and the stampeders shuttled back and forth along the trail, carrying their duffel through the pass to the headwaters of the Yukon.

By the time Hegg reached Dyea, it was too late in the year for him to hope to get down the river to Dawson. He decided to wait on the seaboard side until spring and sell pictures to the men headed across the pass.

Hegg set up a studio in a shack made from the remains of scows that had been smashed on the beach. The shack leaked. It let in both rain and the infrequent bursts of sunlight, and he finally had to put up a tent indoors for use when developing plates.

The best of his Dyea photos show the sweep of the tide-flats, the jackstraw piles of supplies at the edge of town, and the raw board buildings flanking the muddy main street—Trail Street it was rightly called—that led back along the river into the narrowing canyon that rose toward Chilkoot Pass.

Hegg made frequent trips up the trail. The first few miles were deceptively easy. The only real problems were some boulders dropped in the distant past by the glaciers that scoured the valley, a few soft spots in the trail, and the necessity of fording the swift but shallow Dyea at some points.

About five miles back from tidewater an enterprising Irish family named Finigan had built a convenient though precarious bridge, for which they charged whites toll. In time the stampeders became so numerous and bold that

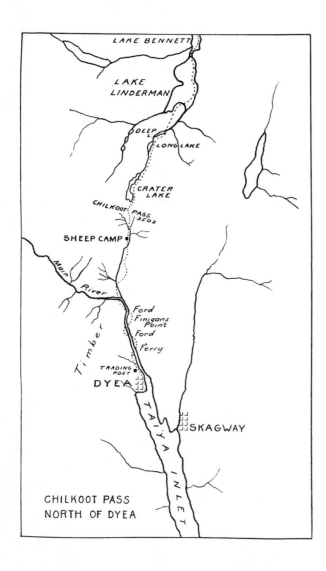

LAKE BENNETT

LAKE LINDERMAN

DEEP L.

LONG LAKE

CRATER LAKE

CHILKOOT PASS 3502

SHEEP CAMP

Man River

Timber River

Ford

Finigans Point

Ford

Ferry

TRADING POST

DYEA

SKAGWAY

TAIYA INLET

CHILKOOT PASS
NORTH OF DYEA

they simply ignored Finigan's demands. He thought it over and opened a bar, for this was an area where, one man noted in a letter home, "a tent, a board counter a foot wide and six-feet long, a long fellow in a Mackinaw coat, and a bottle of whiskey make up a saloon." They named the town after Finigan, and it prospered. A blacksmith set up shop, charging—at peak—ten cents a nail for horseshoeing. Two sisters from Seattle pitched tent and served beans and bacon, bread and butter, dried peaches and coffee for seventy-five cents.

"After five miles of good road," a British officer reported, "hell begins." The terrain was rough, wooded with a tangle of spruce, hemlock, and cottonwood. The trail narrowed, and the hooves of the pack horses and the wheels of wagons chewed the vegetation into a quagmire. To stay on it was to risk bogging down; to leave it was to fight through clutching branches and risk falls on the wet rock.

Dyea Canyon itself was a crevice about two miles long and fifty feet wide at the bottom. The packers shared the bottom with the river. Boulders were piled in dangerous heaps. The grade in places was eighteen degrees. Then, after achieving an elevation of some five hundred feet, the trail dropped slightly to Pleasant Camp. The pleasantness was relative. The camp got its name because a few trees were able to get a living from the rocky ground, and they afforded some shelter.

The more favored stopping point was Sheep Camp, thirteen miles from tidewater. It lay beside the Dyea, milky white here, cold and furiously swift until the freeze. The community consisted of a scattering of tents around a nucleus of two frame buildings and a log cabin set among stunted spruce and hemlock. One of the two board buildings was a hotel. It consisted of a single room, twenty by forty feet, with a calico curtain to shut off the portion where the proprietor and his family lived.

"At noon, but more particularly at evening," said Tappan Adney, the correspondent for *Harper's Weekly*, "the floor of the hotel is crowded by a wild, dirty, wet, unkempt crew of men from Chilkoot, who advance in relays to a long table, where beans, tea and bacon are thrown into them at 75 cents each, payable strictly in advance. When supper is over the floor is thrown open for guests. All who have blankets unroll them and spread them on the floor, take off their socks and shoes and hang them on the rafters, place a coat under their heads and turn in."

It was the last place offering bed and board west of the divide and the Canadian border.

Beyond Sheep Camp horses could not scramble. Nor, in winter, did many men find it worth pulling sleds. The camp was the next to the last staging area for the assault on the summit, four miles distant. From Sheep Camp to the top, it was backpacking all the way. The grade for the first three miles was between twelve and eighteen degrees; it steepened to twenty-five degrees the rest of the way to the little valley known as The Scales; and from there to the summit the grade was thirty degrees. The ascent was 1,950 feet in three miles, then 1,250 feet in the last mile.

The climb was no feat for an alpinist. Women and children crossed the Chilkoot with no complaints other than shortness of breath. But to pack over from twenty to forty times, with the weather changing, the food getting no better, the expenses mounting, time running short, and each load seemingly heavier than the last—that was the challenge of the Chilkoot and the reason that those who met it felt they belonged to a brotherhood.

The first stopping point above Sheep Camp was the Stone House, "so called," said the veteran prospector William Haskell, "because nature seems to have arranged the rocks here with more symmetry than usual, which is saying very little." Next came the long climb to The Scales, where the Chilkats had paused to weigh their loads on a crude balance before starting straight up the mountainside to the notch opening onto the interior. Back and forth from Sheep Camp to The Scales the stampeders trudged until they had their gear assembled below the pass.

Many, looking up, gave up. Equipment was discarded by the ton. Men gladly sold out at a dime on the dollar. The final climb was forbidding enough in summer, when men could zigzag up the mountain. In winter it was hell on ice, a lock-step procession up a flight of twelve hundred steps worn into the frozen snow, the pace of the line determined by the slowest man. To step aside to rest might mean the wait of hours before it was possible to find an opening to get back in line.

There is something of Hieronymous Bosch in Hegg's photos of the scene: the bleak valley, the dark line of men moving up the slope bent under the weight of their packs, the scatter of returnees walking or sliding down the slope to the right on their way back for new burdens.

This was the front line of an army, the assault wave of a combat group without external discipline. Every man was a volunteer. Every man was his own quartermaster. Each had the option of quitting, and there were far more desertions than casualties. But Canadian customs officials, who waited at the summit, reported that forty thousand persons checked through the Chilkoot during the stampede.

In spite of the dangers of the trail, there was only one major disaster. A continuing blizzard in late March and early April of 1898 added two yards of wet snow to the pack on the summit. The Indians saw the danger and withdrew to Dyea. The more knowledgeable Klondikers waited at Sheep Camp. The bold and the foolish camped at The Scales, while those desperately hurried struggled up the ice steps in the coldest hours of early morning when slides were less likely. The nocturnal venturers were right that night was the time to try. It was just before noon, on April third, that the anticipated avalanche poured down from a peak overhanging the trail.

Tons of wet snow covered an area of ten acres to a depth of thirty feet. Several hundred stampeders were entombed. Most clawed their way out, but others found themselves held motionless, cast in the cold concrete of snow.

Men by the hundreds scrambled up from Sheep Camp and Stone House, or down from the summit to dig out the trapped. Hegg, rushing up from tidewater, made the climb to The Scales in a day and photographed the last of the rescue operations. Most of those buried under the avalanche were saved, but sixty-three bodies were taken from the snow. When the ground thawed they were buried in an alpine draw just off the trail. The rush resumed.

Beyond the summit of Chilkoot Pass, it was downhill most of the way to Dawson, though not without danger. Stampeders found the first part of the descent a delight. There was a well-stomped trail to Crater Lake, an expanse of clear ice held in a volcanic goblet. A bar at the lake provided an opportunity to celebrate with supplies that somebody else had packed over the pass, while the lake itself offered easy sailing. Men raised blankets as sails on the sleds they had lugged through the pass, and they made a strange, brave sight as they moved out across the frozen waters. No stranger, though, than Hegg himself, who, on one crossing of the pass, obtained a team of trained goats, which pulled a long sled encumbered not with a blanket sail but with a canvas streamer advertising "Views of Alaska."

Beyond Crater Lake lay Lake Linderman, where many

of the stampeders camped, awaiting the thaw. Those who reached Linderman first had taken most of the trees big enough to provide lumber for boats. Since boats were the next necessity, the majority of the Klondikers who crossed during the winter followed the frozen river out of Linderman to Lake Bennett, where they created a community, built boats, and awaited the thaw on the Yukon.

The harbor at Dyea was shallow. Vessels lay well offshore. Passengers were obliged to make their own arrangements for getting their goods to the beach.

Tides amounting to bores pulsed across the long, muddy beach. It was a race to get the goods above the high-water mark ahead of the rising tide. Teamsters charged twenty dollars an hour when the tide was falling, fifty dollars an hour when the tide was rising.

Each man had to have supplies for a year when he entered Canadian territory. The beachhead at Dyea became an open-air warehouse.

The trail to the pass led by the Healy and Wilson store. Before the stampede it had been the only white residence in the Indian village.

"A trail in Alaska," wrote a man who had just been up the Dyea trail to Chilkoot Pass, "should not be confused with an ordinary highway. . . . It has no further meaning than that a man, and possibly a beast of burden, may travel that way over the natural surface of the ground."

Sheep Camp offered the greatest comfort of any stop along the trail. After a seventy-five cent supper in the hotel, reported a visitor, "all who have blankets unroll them, spread them on the floor, take off their socks and shoes, place a coat under their heads, and turn in."

Above Sheep Camp, beasts of burden were almost useless. It was man-hauling or backpacking the rest of the way to the summit.

At The Scales, the stampeders assembled their gear for the final assault on the summit. Those who could not afford to have their goods carried on the freight cable installed by a Tacoma company had to make twenty or more trips up the twelve hundred steps carved in the ice.

Many looked up, then gave up. Supplies were offered for sale at ten cents on the dollar by those who found the pass too perpendicular.

The line of dark-clad men inched up the mountain at the pace of the slowest climber. A man who stepped aside to rest might wait hours for a chance to get back in line.

The trip down was easier. Some slid on the seats of their pants or rode down on shovels. Others walked down shoulder-deep ruts worn in the snow.

The actual angle of the climb was thirty degrees.

The last few steps seemed straight up.

The actual boundary between the United States and Canada was in dispute. The Canadians established a customs station near the summit (and in doing so seem to have determined the boundary). The Northwest Mounted Police checked each newcomer to be sure he had a year's supplies.

On April 3, 1898, an avalanche poured tons of wet snow onto the trail. "All of a sudden," said a survivor, "I heard a loud report and instantly began to feel myself moving down the hill and, looking round, saw many others suddenly fall down, some with their feet in the air, their heads buried out of sight in the snow."

*Sixty-three bodies were taken from the snow. Many
others were dug out alive. The rush resumed.*

Beyond the summit it was downhill most of the way to Dawson. Crossing Crater Lake was a breeze.

There was even a restaurant at the lake, the first since Sheep Camp. Doughnuts and coffee, one dollar.

Some made camp at Lake Linderman and began to build boats while waiting the thaw.

A tent city sprang up beside the lake.

Others pushed on overland toward Lake Bennett.

The run downstream between the lakes was not a joy ride.

Skagway and the White Pass

ASECOND route led through the mountains from the head of salt water on the Lynn Canal to Lake Bennett, from which the unsalt Yukon descended northward to the golden Klondike. This alternate crossed the White Pass, which—at twenty-nine hundred feet—was lower than Chilkoot, had no upward tilts comparable to the scramble from Stone House to The Scales, let alone from The Scales to the summit on Chilkoot, and was in theory open year-round to pack horses and even wagons.

Only two things were wrong with the White Pass trail. First, it didn't exist. Second, what passed for a trail over the pass debauched into bogland that slushed swampily toward Lake Bennett; and, while difficult when deeply frozen, after the thaw it offered frustrations undreamed of by the tormentors of Tantalus. A man in a race toward a gold field who found himself slowed to a mile a day had cause for dismay.

"The opening of the White Pass as a summer trail was not a blunder, it was a crime," said one of those who had tried to cross it. "When the British Yukon Company was advertising the White Pass Trail and booming its townsite and railway proposition, the trail was not cut out beyond the summit of the pass. There *was* no trail and there has been since no trail but only something that they have called a trail."

Indeed, before the stampede, the Skagway flats did not look good even to the Indians. The very word "Skaguay" connoted north wind—and who was to welcome the cold blast that rolled off the frozen interior? The mountain barrier admittedly added beauty to the Skagway harbor, which was somewhat better protected than the harbor at Dyea, but the winds pervaded the valley like a torment, and the Skagway River was too canyon-bound and rapids-wracked for boats.

The only resident at Skagway when the rush began was Captain William Moore, an elderly and far-sighted adventurer who had made and dissipated several fortunes by providing transportation to earlier gold fields. A man of imagination, Billy Moore had experimented with camels on the paths to the Fraser, but was forced on threat of lynching to abandon the brutes when they spooked the orthodox pack animals. Broke again, Captain Billy had come to Alaska in 1887 with the avowed intention of guessing the route the next gold rush would take and establishing control on its approaches.

Moore decided there would be an important gold strike in the Yukon. He guessed that in any rush, stampeders would find the White Pass attractive. He staked a claim and built a cabin and spent a decade on the chill flats where the tumultuous Skagway River levels out for a rush to the sea.

Captain Moore had guessed right: this *was* the place. Gold *was* found and stampeders *did* arrive. But such were the uncertainties of land titles in the territory at that time

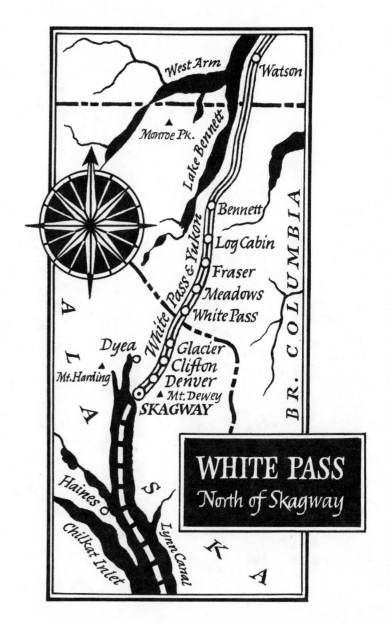

WHITE PASS
North of Skagway

(and indeed, national claim to Skagway harbor, if harbor it was, remained in dispute between Canada and the United States) that the gold rushers, men not beyond avarice, were emboldened to elect a committee to determine, impartially of course, the question of whether Moore or the more recent arrivals had title to the land on which Moore had been living. The committee arrogated title to Moore's claim to the newcomers, and salted the wound by determining that Moore's cabin stood on a public thoroughfare, Main Street no less, and would have to be moved.

Billy Moore eventually won in federal court. Federal judges awarded him 25 per cent of the value of the townsite of Skagway. But by then he didn't need additional old-age security. He had nailed down a new fortune by building a wharf which enabled ships to tie up at Skagway instead of discharging cargoes offshore. The dock not only made Captain Billy rich, it enabled Skagway to surpass rival Dyea.

Also working in Skagway's favor was what Dyea's supporters derided as "the railway proposition." This was the idea that it was possible to lay a line through the coastal mountain barrier to the Yukon drainage basin. It couldn't be done, but the impossible was achieved in little more than a year.

The White Pass and Yukon Railway blossomed from a chance fertilization of capital and energy in dismal Skagway in the early spring of 1898. Sir Thomas Tancrede, pollen rich with British capital, happened to encounter Michael J. Heney, vital with Irish-Canadian energy, in the St. James Hotel, an inelegant, inconvenient but well-patronized barn built largely of corrugated iron and avarice.

Sir Thomas, who had not been impressed by the possibility for profit in pushing rails through the St. Elias Range, was deeply impressed by the Irish Prince, as young Heney was called. The Englishman ticked off the difficulties of construction: hard rock, heavy snow, distant supplies, and a labor force likely to be lured away by rumors of new gold strikes. These obstacles didn't appear Himalayan to Heney. Sir Thomas, who had a theory that a determined man could do anything, finally said, "I'll provide the money and you provide the railway."

Heney, selecting carefully out of the potpourri of men then jammed in Skagway, recruited surveyors willing to rummage the snow-clogged valleys behind the town for the simplest route to the interior. While the survey parties were exploring the possible paths which water and gravity had carved down the mountains, Heney bought several derelict ships stranded along the coast and converted them to barges. As the thaw approached he drew out of the labor supply in town a handful of engineers, then filled up section gangs with men who needed more money to get to the Klondike. A high proportion of Heney's labor gangs were professional men; the White Pass and Yukon Railway had the most overeducated gandy dancers in the history of railroading.

Eric Hegg moved his studio from Dyea to Skagway during the winter of 1897-98. The railroad ran directly in front of his door. He made several trips with the surveying parties and work gangs, though he had left for the Klondike when the actual laying of the track started in July of 1898. (He returned later and pictured the completion of the line.)

Heney had two thousand men at work in the mountains when gold was reported at nearby Atlin in British Columbia. Two thirds of his work force vanished in a week, but somehow he kept construction going. The men had no heavy construction equipment, just black powder and brute power. Most of the grade was across solid granite scoured so smooth by glaciers there was no foothold. The men had to drill holes in the concrete, set crowbars in them, and lay planks on the crowbars to get working space. Often the wind was so strong the men had to be roped to pegs. For one stretch of eighteen miles there was not a wheelbarrowful of gravel or loose earth to be moved; the tracks were set entirely on solid rock or bridges. But by July of 1899 the rails reached as far as Lake Bennett, and the joke that WP&YR stood for "Wait Patiently and You'll Ride" lost its bite.

Among the difficulties surmounted in the construction of the White Pass and Yukon was Jefferson Randolph "Soapy" Smith, a deceptively soft-spoken Georgian who for a few flamboyant months could say of Skagway, "I'm boss of this merry-go-round."

Smith, who had attracted attention as a con man and organizer of rackets in the Rocky Mountain area, migrated to Skagway early in 1898. He came with the intent of becoming boss, an ambition he quickly achieved.

For a bad man, Smith was pretty good. Although one biographer described him as "adept at premature self-defense, with several notches on his revolver," Soapy was essentially an organizer. He was far from money-mad: he simply liked to run things and to be appreciated. He was a self-appointed city manager who specialized in taking over communities where the citizenry was distracted by silver and gold. In return for the right to fleece visitors, Soapy did his best to promote civic improvement and discourage gunplay. He heralded his take-over in Skagway by interrupting a projected lynching with a plea for law and order, emphasizing his point with a Winchester.

Soapy was a sincere advocate of passive resistance, particularly on the part of his victims. He hated a complainer. All he asked was that a customer in one of his saloons or gaming joints take his losses quietly. He exercised no little ingenuity in making his mulcting painless.

There was no cable to Alaska. Soapy opened a "telegraph office" complete except for any method of sending or receiving wires. The clerks accepted messages to any point in the United States at a flat five dollars for ten words. Newcomers marveled at the efficiency of the service. They received replies within a few hours—collect, of course.

The messages filed at the fake telegraph office were taken to Soapy's saloon, known as Jeff's Place, where they were studied for clues as to the amount of money the sender might be carrying. Additional information reached Soapy from steerers, who mingled with the crowds at the dock and picked out the prosperous by their baggage, their talk, and their attire.

Soapy's premier steerer was the "Reverend" Charles Bowers, who promoted himself to "Bishop" during his stay in Skagway. A large, open-faced, sanctimonious thug, Bowers was admired by fellow artists for his skill as a grip man. He had learned the handshakes and distress signals of nearly every secret order in America. Let a mark sport an Elk's tooth, a Masonic square, or the stigmata of any of hundreds of lesser-known orders, and the Reverend Mr. Bowers was kneading the victim's knuckles in the manner approved by bylaw and giving the high sign of the initiate. Bowers introduced his new-met brothers to Skagway businessmen, who offered to let them in on the ground floor of some development so new it was nonexistent.

With most of the suckers killing time in Skagway, Soapy's pains were an extravagance. A high percentage of the migratory males displayed occasional enthusiasm for wine, women, cards, or craps, none in short supply at Jeff's Place. The girls there were experienced, the shell game a sure thing, the dice under control, and the card tables were equipped with an accommodator, an invisible slot through which the dealer could avail himself of an extra ace when the situation demanded.

The backyard at Jeff's Place gave birth to a rare Alaskan euphemism. (Alaska is a land where it is customary to call a spade a steam shovel.) Soapy kept an eagle chained to a perch in the courtyard. Since the area served as a urinal, this decor led those going out back to say they were "going to look at the eagle." If Soapy's men had agreed that a customer was so immune to ordinary temptations that direct action was required, his visit to the courtyard offered the opportunity for sandbagging. In time "seeing the eagle" came to mean being slugged and rolled.

Soapy Smith's suzerainty over Skagway did not deeply concern most of his subjects. They were headed elsewhere, and their attitude was that of men who had been through boot camp or a fraternal hazing: it will make a man of the next fellow to suffer it. Officers of the White Pass and Yukon Railway took a longer view. They felt Soapy was dirtying the name of the White Pass and would make the climb over the Chilkoot attractive. The railway entrepreneurs encouraged attempts by Skagway's "better element" to close the town. Soapy, who had been through reforms before, countered the organization of a clean-up committee of 101 by announcing the formation of a law-and-order organization of 303 members. Reformers decided not to buck those odds.

Out on the trail to the pass, where the work of laying

rails was in progress, Heney was able to enforce his rule of "No liquor in camp." When work started at Rocky Point, one of Soapy's gang set up a gambling and drinking tent nearby. Heney ordered him away but he refused to go. Heney sent for Mike Foy, the camp foreman, and pointed to a big rock on the cliff above the tent saloon. "That rock has to be out of there by five tomorrow morning, not a minute later," he said.

Soapy's minion decided Heney was bluffing and went to bed. The next morning Foy sent a rock gang to put a few sticks of dynamite in the rock, then dispatched a man to wake up the slumbering barkeep. He still thought it was a bluff.

Foy went to the tent himself. "In one minute," he said, "I'm giving the order to touch off the fuse. It will then burn for one minute and that rock will arrive here or hereabouts."

"Aw, go to hell," said the barkeep.

"Fire," Foy called to the crew and ran for cover. He was joined behind a sheltering point of rock by the barkeep, clad only in long johns and considerably impressed. The dynamite went off. The rock smashed the tent and the store of liquor.

Foy reported back to Heney. "That rock is down, sir."

"Where's the man?"

"The last I saw of him he was going down the trail in his underclothes, cursing."

"That's all right," said Heney.

But back in town Soapy was still supreme. When Congress declared war on Spain on April 24, 1898, Smith set himself up as captain of Company A, First Regiment, Alaskan National Guard, and wrote the Secretary of War offering himself and his men for duty overseas. The Secretary wrote back declining the offer but praising Soapy's patriotism.

That Smith was sincerely patriotic seems probable; that he was still opportunistic, certain. The creation of the guard unit gave him the opportunity to march his henchmen, armed, through the streets of the town. And he could not resist the temptation to profit from the patriotism of others. He set up a fake army recruiting office where volunteers had their pockets picked while they underwent physical examinations, which they invariably failed.

Soapy distributed resplendent badges on behalf of the Skagway Military Company, Jeff R. Smith, Captain, urging that the *Maine* be remembered and Cuba freed. On May Day he organized the biggest parade Alaska had seen and presided over a formal hanging in effigy of the commander of Spanish forces in Cuba. He was elected by popular vote to serve as Grand Marshal of the Fourth of July parade and, his black beard combed and pomaded, his black hat tilted jauntily, he rode the streets on a white horse. Occasionally he paused to give candy to the children.

This moment of greatest pride came just before the fall.

While Smith showed a growing interest in popular esteem, his gang members were getting out of control. One was believed to have murdered a young woman who tired of his advances; another to have shot, unnecessarily, a youth in an argument over the relative merits of the White Pass and Chilkoot trails. Then, on July 7, J. D. Stewart arrived in town.

Stewart was a prospector, a young Canadian, beefy and stolid. He was an authentic sourdough who had gone in the year before, seen the Yukon freeze, waited out the thaw, and now was coming Outside with a year's collection of dust and nuggets. He hadn't struck it rich, but the accumulation of gold in his poke was worth something like twenty-eight hundred dollars.

The only surviving photograph of Stewart—not by Hegg —indicates that he did not radiate brightness. He was a bumpkin who wore a cap too small and an expression too challenging: "Just try to put something over on me!" it seems to say. Inevitably he found his way to Soapy's saloon. He emerged broke.

Poor Stewart had not even been given the illusion of opportunity. No card sharp offered him a few winning hands, no bar hustler offered willing arms. As soon as he produced his poke some fellow grabbed it and ran, somebody else held him up accidentally as he started in pursuit, and the most he could get out of the management was the address of the United States Deputy Marshal, the designated receptacle for complaints. Stewart complained and the marshal, who was a well-oiled cog in the Smith apparatus, said that since he couldn't identify the culprit the best thing for him to do would be to climb back over the mountains and get some more nuggets and dust. Stewart could see that if he had to come out by way of Skagway this might be a waste of time. He went around town complaining.

As the story of Stewart's misadventure in Jeff's Place spread, so did concern. The "better element" was already unhappy about stories circulating in West Coast seaports about Soapy's operations. And indeed some tales were fanciful even beyond the wildness of reality. But now, the business people of Skagway suddenly realized, if Soapy's skinning of suckers headed inland had given the town a bad name, worse would follow the robbery of the outward bound. They would soon be Outside and intent on ruining what reputation Skagway had left. Victims like Stewart would soon be south and subject to interviews. The call was sounded for the mustering of a vigilance committee.

There followed a crescendo of confrontations, a clangor of demands for the return of Stewart's gold and denials of its possession or existence, meetings loudly infiltrated by Soapy's followers or interrupted by Captain Smith's personal and armed appearance, a slow, reluctant stiffening of community will, a final assembly of those determined to clean up the town, and a moment of purest melodrama, with Soapy Smith, somewhat drunk and very alone, deaf to warnings from friends, walking down the very street up which he had led the Fourth of July parade, determined to face down those who challenged his reign.

Soapy, at the end of his walk, and his life, found himself face to face with an old friend, Frank Reid, a brave, flabby man who, but for this encounter, would have been remembered only as the city engineer designate who drew up the plan for Skagway which, illegally, deprived first settler Billy Moore of his claim. Smith and Reid knew each other well. Legend says each had a reluctant admiration for the other's strengths. But now, in the paleness of the July night, Reid blocked Soapy's path to the meeting. Reid held a six-shooter. Smith was festooned with a derringer and a Colt .45, and was holding a Winchester rifle.

Accounts differ on what happened when the old friends met. There are more versions of the encounter than there were actual witnesses. Certainly Reid tried to block Smith from reaching the warehouse where the vigilantes were meeting. Both men fired, both fell, both died—Smith instantly, a bullet in his heart, Reid after more than a week of agony from a shot in the abdomen.

In death, Jefferson Randolph Smith was almost unmourned. Skagway's attention centered first on rounding up and deporting Soapy's henchmen, then on honoring Reid. It was probably inevitable, though, that with the passage of time the legend of Soapy Smith, the ultimate con man, has come to be one of Skagway's most exploitable community assets, and a reconstructed Jeff's Place a tourist attraction.

Four photos of Soapy Smith are known to exist. One shows him standing in a bar placed either in Creede, Colorado, or in Skagway; another catches him on horseback in the Fourth of July parade; the other two show him dead. Of these, only one of the morgue shots was in Eric Hegg's files. It shows Dr. B. F. Whiting, chief surgeon for the White Pass and Yukon Railway, removing the bullet from Smith's body. Another picture in the Hegg files is of Frank Reid, dying in bed in his cabin after the duel. It is unlikely that Hegg took either picture. Photographers of the day copied each other's prints without hesitation. The shots may even have been taken by whatever photographer ran Hegg's studio after he had started across the trail for Dawson. In any case, dates on other pictures indicate that Hegg was on the Yukon River when Soapy was killed.

Skagway's great advantages over Dyea as a gateway to the Klondike were the existence of wharves and the rumor of a trail suitable for pack animals.

The Al-Ki *was the first vessel to leave Seattle for the North after the* Portland *brought in its "ton of gold."*

The Mercury, *stranded in a gale, was reduced to barge service.*

The Resolute *was brought up from Yaquina Bay to tow barges and sailing vessels.*

A town sprang up on the flats. It looked orderly but according to the super-intendent of the Northwest Mounted Police was "little better than a hell on earth . . . about the roughest place in the world."

A city hall was built and a city government established.

But for some months the seat of power was Jeff's Place, a saloon and gaming joint that served as headquarters for Jefferson "Soapy" Smith and his gang.

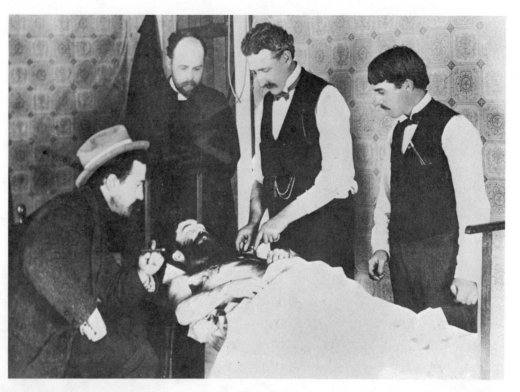

Soapy was killed in a shoot-out with Frank Reid, the city engineer, when he tried to crash a vigilante meeting held in his honor. F. B. Whiting, surgeon for the White Pass and Yukon Railway, performs the autopsy.

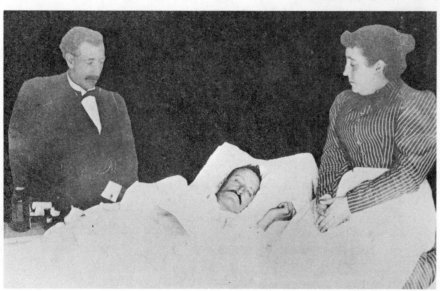

Reid died several days later, a hero to the townsfolk.

Rails were laid from the waterfront toward the White Pass, but for the first two years of the rush, dogs and horses hauled the freight. Hegg's Skagway studio is in the center background.

Matched teams of malemutes were a rarity during the rush. Any dog strong enough to pull was put in harness. Departure was an occasion. Here a bagpiper serenades a party of Presbyterian missionaries.

The first few miles along the Skagway River were relatively easy.

Trouble began where giant boulders con-
stricted the trail. Horses had to be goaded
over the ledges.

The stampeders claimed that the three-note song of the golden crowned sparrows on White Pass was "I'm so tired."

The narrow trail caused huge traffic jams. Starving horses nipped hay from the bales being hauled in for fodder.

Many horses were abandoned by their owners. "Their hearts turned to stone—those which did not break—and they became beasts, the men on the Dead Horse Trail," wrote Jack London.

Captain Arthur H. Lee of the Royal Military College, Kingston, Ontario, wrote of the Dead Horse Trail: "To put it very mildly, it's a hell of a business."

The trail was cluttered with cached goods and abandoned sleds.

The White Pass summit as seen from Cutoff Canyon.

Snowstorm on the summit. "The man who travels in Alaska only when the weather is good will make about a mile a month," said a veteran prospector. "And it is a country of magnificent distances."

From the summit the trail to the lakes was passable in winter, a quagmire after the thaw. "To call it a year-round trail was not a mistake, it was a crime," said one reporter.

The Canadian customs were at Log Cabin.

The trail might be terrible but the scenery was superb: Mount Halcon from Log Cabin.

Tagish Charley, who was with George Carmack when he discovered gold on the Klondike, is shown here hauling supplies on the White Pass trail.

Everybody dreamed of the day when steam would replace
muscle for moving goods across the mountains.

Surveyor Strong at work between Summit and Log Cabin.

No heavy construction equipment was available. The men moved mountains with black powder and pry-bars.

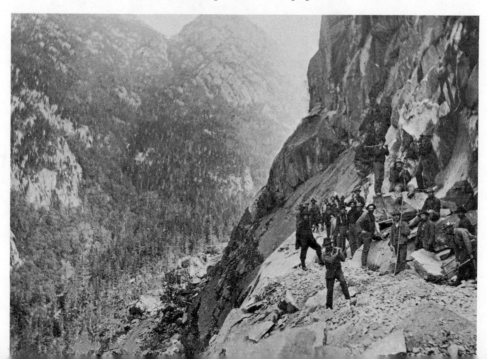

Wooden trestles carried the rails across the gorges. There was only one tunnel.

When blizzards struck, everyone helped clear the track.

Driving the last spike. President S. H. Graves invited one of the American dig-
nitaries to swing the sledge. He bent the golden spike double.

Train returning to tidewater.

Down the Yukon

THE chain of lakes which caught the snow melt from the interior slopes of the Chilkoot and White passes drained into the Yukon. Stampeders who made it across the passes during the freeze pitched their tents along the lakes; waiting the thaw, they constructed boats to use on the long descent to Dawson City.

While still in Dyea, Hegg had been joined by his brother Pete and by W. B. Anderson, another Scandinavian from Whatcom. Anderson, a tall man with a drooping mustache, was expert with tools; he had worked as a logger, a carpenter, and a butcher. The men entered an agreement to pool their resources. Anderson and young Hegg would cross the mountains and build a boat for the run down the Yukon; Eric Hegg would stay behind and earn money making pictures.

A few Klondikers carried prefabricated boats over the passes. Others lugged boards, though packers charged premium rates for lumber. There was a small sawmill at Lake Bennett—"a steam-driven gold-mine," some called it—but it could not meet the demand for lumber. Young Hegg and Anderson had to cut their own.

They started by selecting suitable trees. Two logs were sufficient if they would cut into nine-inch boards, but Lake Linderman and Lake Bennett were near the timber line and most trees were too small. Once trees were located and the logs cut, the boat builders erected a saw-pit. These pits were simple but sturdy frames of logs on which the saw log could be rested. Putting them up required more sweat than artistry.

When the saw-pit was ready, skids were leaned against it and the saw log rolled up the skids and its ends settled in notches on the top. The bark and sapwood were skinned off, and slabs marked out with a chalk line. Then the men went to work with a whipsaw, a long, coarse-toothed instrument tapering to one end, with handles fixed to each end at right angles.

The whipsaw was part of the Klondike experience. Sourdoughs claimed it ended more good friendships than any institution except marriage. "It should be suppressed," said one. "No character is strong enough to withstand it. Two angels could not saw their first log with one of these things without getting into a fight. It is more trying than the Chilkoot pass."

As the stampeders worked, members of the Northwest Mounted Police moved through the chaos of improvisation giving counsel. "Make the boats long and strong," they said. "The Yukon is both." Similar advice was found in the December 15 edition of the Dawson City *News*, which circulated in the camps. "Boats should be about 18 to 22 feet long. Make them strong. Take your time. Alaska and the Klondike are big and gold has no legs."

Besides giving advice on boat building, the paper, which

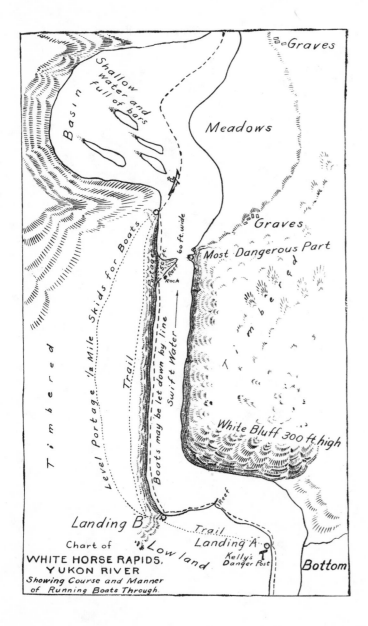

Chart of
WHITE HORSE RAPIDS,
YUKON RIVER
Showing Course and Manner
of Running Boats Through.

was read to tatters, described "the ten greatest dangers of the trip to the Klondike," a compendium of risks climaxed by the rapids at White Horse. Voyagers memorized the description like a catechism:

"The rapids are about a half-mile long and the only dangerous point is at the very foot, where there is a reef of rock that makes out from the left shore. It narrows the stream from 160 feet to less than half that distance. The waters boil considerable at this reef and the waves run from two to five feet high. A short boat bobs about at the mercy of these waves. Here a long boat, 18 to 22 feet, comes in handy. The landing to the left is below the reef and over to the right opposite this landing are graves of those who drowned in the attempt to shoot White Horse Rapids."

At Lake Bennett, Anderson and Pete Hegg teamed up with a former whaleman named Snow, another able practitioner with saw and axe. They whipsawed boards and built two good boats, one with a small cabin forward which could be used as a darkroom.

There were ten thousand men at Bennett, ten thousand at Linderman, and twenty thousand shuttling their goods up the trails from Dyea and Skagway when Hegg joined the party sometime in May. He operated a studio in the tent town, but when the ice broke on the lake on May 29, he turned it over to Edward J. Hamacher (who was to become one of the leading photographers of the Yukon Territory) and joined the fantastic flotilla headed north.

Seven thousand one hundred and twenty-four boats, by Mounted Police count, started down the river: skiffs and scows and canoes and barges and kayaks, boats of canvas and boats of balsa, boats that had been screwed together and boats that had been glued together, boats that looked like packing boxes and boats that looked like coffins, and might well be.

The run north was an alternation of work, discomfort, and danger, the three elements often combining. The boats were overloaded; the Mounties at the station at the foot of Lake Marsh would turn back any man who did not have seven hundred pounds of grub, and thirty million pounds of food were floated down to Dawson in the first months of summer. The winds were strong, usually adverse, and often dangerous. There were long stretches of slack water through which the boats had to be rowed, sailed, poled, or dragged. Sometimes ice floes poured out from the tributaries. Where the river ran free, it was dangerously fast. There were snags and sandbars to be avoided and rapids that could be avoided only by back-breaking portages.

And there were the mosquitoes.

Even Lake Bennett was dangerous. It was twenty-five miles long, narrow at the upper end but about five miles wide to the north. The winds—prevailing from the north in the early summer—kicked up a chop that threatened boats loaded so heavily they had only inches of freeboard. In a following wind, when the blanket sails were spread on the crude masts, the man at the tiller oar had to fight every minute to keep the craft from veering ashore. "Cap'n" Snow, the old whaleman, rigged a canvas wave catcher at the bow of Hegg's boat, and it proved helpful.

The lake narrowed into a stream, the stream opened onto Tagish Lake, a spangle of inlets down which winds rushed treacherously. There were said to be more drownings off Big Windy Arm than at White Horse Rapids. The Hegg party made it through without incident.

A slow, shallow stream about six miles long led to bog-like Lake Marsh. The lake was so shallow that it was the last to break in the thaw, and here Hegg was to take a series of eerie pictures of boats maneuvering through the floes.

Twenty-three miles below Lake Marsh, after a run down swift water, they came to Miles Canyon, second only to White Horse in ill repute. The current strengthened, and the dull roar of rapids pulsed up to the voyagers. At a bend a flag of red cloth warned of danger, and a sign painted on a board said "CANNON." The river constricted to about a hundred feet between walls of sheer, black basalt. The water piled up in midstream. The trick was to ride the hogback about halfway through the canyon, then veer off toward the right to avoid an immense whirlpool that spun to portside, then to regain the center and stay in midstream almost to the foot of the canyon, where it was best to fight right again to avoid the large rock that speared up dead center in the stream.

There were professional pilots at Miles, but a dour note in one guidebook suggested "Select a man with references, if possible." The Hegg party went through on their own.

The best thing about White Horse Rapids, which lay just below, was that only an idiot could blunder into them by mistake. A blaze of pale rock striped the basalt cliff and marked the approach to the canyon. There was always a motley of boats pulled onto the left bank, while their owners weighed the costs in time and dollars of portaging against the risk of trying to ride out the rapids.

"Go get a good view of the rapids and then decide whether you will portage," a popular guidebook urged. Those who walked along the trail down to the left bank passed notes of triumph and encouragement tacked to blazes in trees or broken oars:

> Sept. 8, 1897. Boat Cora and Meda 20 ft long 8 ft 3 in beam, 26 in. deep. safely shot the White Horse Rapids loded with 4000 pounds.

And,

> Gudmond Jensen
> G. G. Tripp
> Tom
> Mike went
> threw all right.

But farther on they saw beyond the fang of the reef the waves, towering, white-crested, and so close together that any boat overloaded or poorly handled was still nose-down after the first wave and was swallowed by the second. During the first days of the 1898 rush, 150 boats were sunk or smashed. Samuel Benton Steele, the towering superintendent of the Northwest Mounted Police, with more firmness than legal authority, imposed rules for the rapids. No women were to try the river. All boats must be inspected. Only experienced boatsmen could try to go through.

The Hegg party portaged one boat along the tramway of wood rails a young man named Norman Macaulay was building across the five-mile portage. The other they ran through. Apparently they stayed at the rapids for several days, with Hegg carrying his camera to various points from which he could photograph boats breasting the waves, while Anderson worked for Macaulay on the tramway.

Below the White Horse Rapids it was clear sailing until they reached Lake LeBarge, a long, misleading body where the current lured unwary boatsmen to the east shore, which was lined with cliffs and offered no landing spots when the sudden and frequent squalls swept the lake.

LeBarge emptied into Thirty Mile River, a stretch noted for being swift, crooked, and full of rocks. Past the Hootalinqua they floated, past the Big Salmon and the Little Salmon, to the Five Finger Rapids, a barrier beautiful and dangerous. This was only a little more than halfway to the Klondike—316 miles from the head of Lake Bennett, still

244 from Dawson—but beyond Five Finger Rapids there was just Rink Rapids and then the broad, open water of the main stem.

Though the danger was past, discomfort was not. This was the worst of the mosquito country. Klondikers came to welcome rain as an insect repellent and to invent stories about Yukon mosquitoes that carried off eagles as food for their young. At Stewart City, where there were some amenities, a man could relax in the knowledge that the goal was only eighty miles ahead, but the irritation of the mosquitoes was so great that more parties dissolved in dispute here than anywhere else on the river.

The Hegg party survived intact. At Stewart City they heard that lumber was in great demand at Dawson, where an American who had a concession on timber rights for five miles along the Klondike was subletting the right to cut wood at five dollars a cord. They stayed long enough for Anderson to make up two rafts of logs, which they towed the rest of the way north.

It was early July when, over a cluster of islands, they caught a glimpse of a few tents high up on a hillside, and beyond them the huge gray slide of rock and gravel called The Moosehide. They rode the swift, yellow-gray flood around a great bend, then fought their way over to the right bank and up into the dark waters of the Klondike.

So this was Dawson, the golden city; or—as others put it—a rectangle in a bog.

Long before the railroad reached Lake Bennett, a town grew up.

There were three hotels, a bakery, a restaurant, a photo studio. But Bennett's streets were best navigated in a cross between a boat and a sled.

The main occupation of the stampeders during the winter was sawing boards and building boats. Of the whipsaw it was said, "Two angels could not saw their first log with one of these things and not get into a fight."

The ice broke on May 29, 1898. Within the week more than a thousand boats started downstream.

There was little current in the lakes but sudden storms made the waters dangerous. At Windy Arm on Lake Tagish the prudent kept close to shore.

In the slow waters of Fifty Mile River some raised sail. A lucky group of Canadians caught a tow.

Ice clogged Lake Marsh, a shallow body of water. Hegg took these eerie pictures on a foggy day in 1899.

The first dangerous rapids were at Miles Canyon. The voyagers landed above the rapids to debate the best way of running the white water.

A boat entering Miles Canyon was kept in midriver, where the water piled up a yard higher than along the banks. Just beyond the curve lay a huge whirlpool.

Next came Squaw Rapids, which were considered a warm-up for White Horse.

"The rapids are about a half-mile long," said one guidebook of White Horse. "The only dangerous point is at the very foot where there is a reef or rock that makes out from the left shore. . . . The waters boil considerable at this reef, and the waves run from two to five feet high."

The Mane of the Horse. "Go and get a good view of the rapids and then decide whether you will portage."

Even craft that got through the rapids might have taken on so much water that they would sink in the calm waters below. This scow was lucky. Somebody got a line out to it and hauled it ashore.

The Canyon and White Horse Rapids Tramway ran on wooden rails around the rapids. To use it was a sign of affluence, not cowardice.

The Hegg party at the mouth of Stewart River. The danger was past but not the discomfort—note the mosquito nets. "One good thing about a rainstorm," a Klondiker said in a letter home, "is the repulsion that exists between a moving drop of water and a comparatively stationary mosquito. . . ."

Five Finger Rapids were more beautiful than dangerous—unless the helmsman had to dispute passage with a steamer being roped upstream.

The Yukon could be serene.

Dawson

ONLY two years earlier this land at the juncture of the rivers had been a moose pasture, true wilderness, back of beyond. Some twenty miles away stood the Dome, the highest mountain in the area, 4,250 feet above sea level, 3,050 feet above the confluence of the Klondike and the Yukon, a wrinkled breast of a mountain, more beautiful to look from than at.

In August of 1896 an American prospector had stood on the heights and studied the watershed. "Below and far in the distance," George Washington Carmack wrote later, "I saw the low hills rolling and undulating in great windrows of living colors; the tops of the bald hills seemed to be painted in bands and stripes of green, yellow and red, showing that they were highly mineralized. Far back in the blue distance, close to the sky, towered the huge battlements of the Rockies, as though acting as bulwark for the protection of their offspring."

Carmack was a strange one, more moose hunter than prospector, more interested in the silver of salmon than the glint of gold. Perhaps he had read a lesson in his father's life: the elder Carmack joined the rush to California in '49 but died broke. Young Carmack had come north in 1885 to prospect but took to the Indian life and spent more time fishing than panning.

He built a cabin near Five Finger Rapids, where he lived

with his Indian wife, and read the *Scientific American* and wrote occasional poetry. Such was his make-up that when, a few days before climbing the Dome, he dreamed of a salmon with gold pieces for eyes and nuggets for teeth he took it as a sign that he should go fishing.

But Carmack's disinterest in gold was not total. He had come to the Klondike on a tip from Robert Henderson, a spare, dour Canadian, who told of finding strong evidence of gold on another creek that drained off the Dome. After climbing down from the Dome, Carmack and two Indian companions paused to rest near the point where a stream known as Rabbit Creek ran into the Klondike. Looking down at the stream, Carmack saw a long narrow strip of bedrock just under the water.

"I reached down and picked up a nugget about the size of a dime," he recalled later. "I put it between my teeth and bit at it like a newsboy who had found a quarter in the street. Looking up at my two companions, I held up the nugget between thumb and forefinger and shouted 'Hi Yu, gold! Bring down the pan and shovel. Hi Yak.'

"I took the shovel and dug up some of the loose bed-rock. In turning over some of the flat pieces I could see the raw gold laying thick between the flaky slabs like cheese sandwiches. Putting some of the broken bed-rock into the pan I washed it down and got about a quarter of an ounce, mostly coarse gold. . . .

"We did a war dance around that pan . . . a combination

war dance, composed of a Scotch hornpipe, Indian fox trot, syncopated Irish jig and a sort of Siwash hula-hula. Then we sat down to rest and smoke."

The Indians were later to claim that they had made the first discovery and that they had to wake Carmack to tell him about it. No matter. This was the richest gold strike ever made. It was to change the history of Alaska, western Canada, and the Pacific Northwest.

Carmack says he renamed the Rabbit as Bonanza then and there (others take credit for this, too), measured out two claims for himself (the second being allowed by right of discovery), and a claim for each of his two Indian companions, then started down the Yukon to Forty Mile to record his claim at the police post. Somehow he neglected to tell Bob Henderson, who was camped not far away, that his tip had been a good one. This discourtesy may have stemmed from Henderson's earlier rudeness to Carmack's Indian in-laws.

Carmack held out on no one else. He felt he had "just dealt myself a royal flush in the game of life, and the whole world was a jack-pot." He told everyone he met on the way of his discovery, and those who believed him and acted on his advice became rich. And when he went into Bill McPhee's saloon at Forty Mile, knocked back two whiskeys, and glowing with beneficence told of his strike and backed his words by pouring from a cartridge the rough flakes he'd panned from the Bonanza, the stampede started.

This was what prospecting was about. The chance of getting rich by finding an original strike was far less than the chance of getting rich by being nearby when someone else made a find and thus being able to stake an adjoining claim. No telegraph wires ran through the wilderness, but the word spread, the word that Stick George, Siwash George, yes, old Lying George Carmack had found gold on the Klondike. It emptied the camps like Forty Mile. It drew the old-timers from the remote streams. It caused merchants and missionaries and saloonkeepers to lock the doors of their establishments and head for the new diggings.

Within two weeks, Bonanza was staked its entire distance in a welter of conflicting claims, and men were probing other streams in the area. On the last day of August, Antone Stander, a twenty-nine-year-old ex-cowboy from Austria, who had been roaming the Yukon country for two years in unsuccessful search of gold, knelt by the south fork of the Bonanza, a tributary of the tributary, a trickle of dark water that flowed in from the far side of the Dome and had been dismissed as Bonanza's pup by more experienced prospectors. From his first pan Stander took six dollars' worth of coarse gold grains. He and his four companions paced out claims that were each to yield more than a million dollars, and the pup became known as Eldorado.

The Klondike was even more of a lottery than most strikes. The topography was deceptive, and gold lay con-

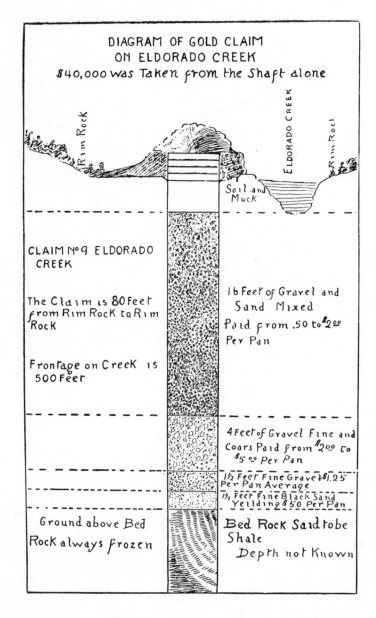

DIAGRAM OF GOLD CLAIM
ON ELDORADO CREEK
$40,000 was Taken from the Shaft alone

Rim Rock

ELDORADO CREEK

Rim Rock

Soil and Muck

CLAIM Nº9 ELDORADO CREEK

The Claim is 80 Feet from Rim Rock to Rim Rock

Frontage on Creek is 500 Feet

Ground above Bed Rock always frozen

16 Feet of Gravel and Sand Mixed Paid from .50 to $2.00 Per Pan

4 Feet of Gravel Fine and Coars Paid from $2.00 to $5.00 Per Pan

1½ Feet Fine Gravel $1.25 Per Pan Average
1½ Feet Fine Black Sand Yeilding $.50 Per Pan

Bed Rock Said to be Shale
Depth not Known

centrated in improbable places. "You're more likely to find it where it ain't than where it is," the saying went. The cheechako had equal chance with the sourdough.

What was being found was surface gold, profuse enough to make a man well to do, but no proof that enormous riches lay below. The only way to determine what a prospect was really worth was to get down to bedrock. That meant digging—slow, discouraging, often fruitless digging through the permafrost.

To sink a shaft through the frozen earth of the subarctic, it was necessary first to thaw the ground. That meant logging the nearby streams or going up the mountainside to cut firewood and packing it to the claim. Then a hole was scraped in the surface moss and debris and a fire built on the cleared surface. When the fire died, the ashes and thawed dirt were dug out and another fire built. The process was repeated until bedrock was reached. The average rate of descent was about a foot a day. Bedrock lay from five to twenty-five feet down.

After a prospector reached bedrock, he began "drifting." That is, he built his next fire at the side of the shaft in what seemed to him the most promising direction and kept thawing and shoveling and hauling out the muck until he found what he was looking for or gave up. "There is no doubt," reported William Ogilvie, the dominion land surveyor, "that this is the hardest country in the history of mining in which to prospect."

Throughout the first winter, during the long nights when the temperatures hung in the minus sixties and the great stars blazed overhead and the northern lights flared, when it was so cold and still the camp dogs shied from the spark of a touch, the rich, sweat-crusted, scurvy-plagued prospectors grubbed in their holes, piling up fortunes in dirty gravel outside cabins less commodious than kennels, and dreaming of spring when the streams would run again and there would be water for sluicing.

Most of the lumber for sluice boxes had to be whipsawed, though Joe Ladue, a shrewd backwoods merchant and promoter, had immediately brought in a mill and set it up on

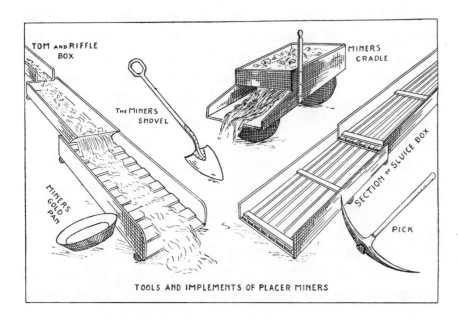

TOOLS AND IMPLEMENTS OF PLACER MINERS

the townsite he staked out at the mouth of the Klondike and called Dawson City after George M. Dawson, a government geologist. The mill couldn't keep up with the demand for boards for commercial buildings, let alone sluices, nor could most of the prospectors afford the luxury of sawed wood.

The boxes were usually about ten inches high and twelve or fourteen inches across the bottom. They varied in length according to the number of men working the diggings and the amount of muck to be washed, but usually ran about fifty feet for two men. Across the bottom lay successive riffles. These were small, round poles set lengthwise in frames so that they lay an inch and a half or two inches apart. At the lower end of the box was another set of riffles with slats about an inch square. When the streams thawed in the spring, water was diverted to the sluices. The pay dirt, hauled up during the winter's grubbing, was shoveled in. The earth was washed away, the gold and small gravel settled in the riffles. The catch in the tail riffles was then panned for gold.

During that first frozen, fantastic winter after Carmack's strike, men became millionaires—but millionaires in frozen muck, millionaires short of cash in a town short of goods. Carmack himself worked at Ladue's mill to pay for material he needed to work his claim.

Nobody starved, but scurvy claimed some and crippled others; alcohol, far more. Tensions rose as the winter wore on. The Mounties permitted no men to carry sidearms; there were no shootings, but fights were not unknown, even among Dawson's female population. A surviving copy of the town's first handwritten newspaper carries the good word that Mountain Molly had regained the consciousness she lost when brained with a bottle by a colleague during an argument over a customer. "Women are few and we can't spare any," the editor cautioned.

During the summer of 1897, Dawson received a replenishment of women, mining equipment, food, and other necessities. Even before the *Portland* and the *Excelsior* carried the first beneficiaries of Carmack's strike Outside and made the rush world-wide, prospectors from Alaska and British Columbia began arriving. The likely creek beds were claimed their full length several times over, and the late-comers spread over the countryside scraping and digging.

A pair of veteran Scandinavian prospectors, Nathan Kresge and Nels Peterson, noted that high on the benchland above Bonanza, where diggers had denuded the hills of their protective cover of trees, the spring rains sometimes exposed patches of white gravel. Since this was considered a sign of gold in the stream beds, they started digging and panning high up on the ridge, to the brief amusement of the conventional. Thus the riches of French Hill were uncovered.

A raw tenderfoot named Oliver Millett, who had quit

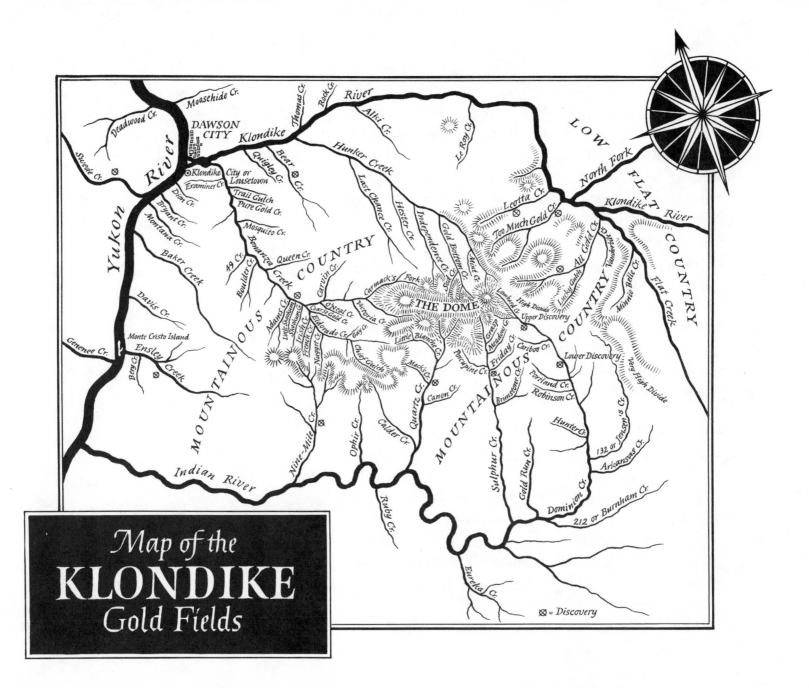

Map of the
KLONDIKE
Gold Fields

⊗ = Discovery

his job on the green chain of a Seattle sawmill the day the *Portland* arrived, reached Dawson in October of 1897. Unhampered by experience he studied the lay of the land, guessed out the course of the long-dead stream that had brought down the riches of Eldorado and Bonanza, and on a claim derisively called Cheechako Hill unearthed the last of the great strikes.

By the time Hegg and his party arrived in July of 1898, the era of discovery had ended (though rumors and rushes still occurred), and the period of exploitation and development was in full flower. Forty thousand persons were in, or about, Dawson by the end of summer. More poured off each southbound steamer and northbound scow. Joe Ladue was getting five thousand dollars a front foot for his best lots, and the nonproducers (as miners called everyone from ministers to reporters) were battening off the golden overflow from the claims.

Dawson was a town where everybody soon knew everybody, and anybody's business was everybody's business; a town 90 per cent American in population but under Canadian law; a community where some officials were maligned as corrupt but a few, like William Ogilvie, the dominion surveyor, showed rectitude beyond the demand of any rule except a good man's conscience. Most of all, Dawson was a town where the chaos of individual panning was being institutionalized into the production of gold. This was a phenomenon Hegg was experienced in photographing.

He set up a studio in a cabin with log walls and a tent roof, which he boarded over when he found the time and money. He was in and out of Dawson for the next three years and recorded the change from tent town to clapboard metropolis. He pictured its celebrations and its fires. He photographed the official thermometer stuck at minus sixty-eight one January and the townsfolk at work under the midnight sun in June. He aimed his camera at laundresses and society women, at dance hall girls and the dreary whores who were banished to a line of cribs outside town, because they offered a threat not to the town's morals but to its fire protection.

Some of the time Hegg worked alone. Occasionally he collaborated with Edward P. Larrs and Joseph E. N. Duclos, who also maintained a studio in Dawson. Thus he was able to make frequent trips out to the gold fields, where he photographed not only the mines and cabins and the proliferation of sluices but the roadhouses that blossomed beside the trails, and the growth of a transportation complex. He also made a few trips back to Skagway and one Outside, during which he went to New York. On his return he liked to tell the sourdoughs of a carriage jam he caused on Fifth Avenue when he exhibited pictures of the climb over the Chilkoot Pass.

When the men reached Dawson they usually lived beside their boats for a few days until they decided whether to work for somebody else or try their luck on the still unclaimed streams.

"It is all unreal," said the correspondent of the London Chronicle. "A sawboard metropolis where no town should be. Daylight at midnight. Millionaires too occupied to bathe." Hegg took this picture of the mouth of the Klondike at midnight.

Unclaimed wilderness in 1896, Dawson in 1898 was the largest city in Canada west of Winnipeg and only slightly smaller than Seattle, Portland, or Tacoma. It was a city of movement, and the movement was toward the gold fields.

The Bartlett brothers were among the prime movers. They had hauled goods across the White Pass and the Chilkoot until they realized that the railroad would ruin that business. They shipped their wheels and animals down the Yukon, and for several years dominated transport between Dawson and the diggings.

Bonanza! The cabin in the left foreground is almost on the spot where Carmack discovered gold. Gold Hill humps to the right. The mouth of Eldorado Creek lies behind the hill.

Too late to stake on Bonanza, the Nova Scotian Oliver Millett deduced that the gold had been carried down the left bank by an ancient stream. He was correct. Cheechako Hill was named in derision for a tenderfoot, but is remembered in legend as one of the richest strikes.

Through the winter they dug. They thawed the ground with bonfires, shoved up dirt until they came to the old stream bed, and then brought up the gold-laced dirt in buckets. The frozen muck, worth millions, waited to be washed when the streams thawed.

*They slept atop riches in cabins the poorest at home might scorn. This
one stood on the sixth claim upstream from Carmack's.*

They dug down through the frozen soil, then began drifting in the direction they believed most golden.

Lumber was nearly as precious as metal. It was needed for fires, for shoring up the face, for building cabins.

It took an expert's eye to trace the course of a long-buried stream that had washed gold toward the Klondike.

There were few prizes for being second in a gold rush. These men were employees, grubbing gold for *wages*.

The gold-laced rubble was raised by windlass and dumped in piles to be washed later.
This claim was on French Hill, above Tom Lippy's claim on Eldorado.

Inside the cabins, Klondikers checked the content of the dirt they were working. The can behind the stovepipe contains sourdough pancake batter.

There might be a million in gold in the dirt at the pit head but dinner was a slab of bread chopped from a frozen loaf and gnawed by candlelight.

When spring came and the streams flowed, the water was diverted through sluices and used to wash the gold in a series of rockers.

The lone men longed for women.

And enterprising women knew what they wanted.

Belinda Mulrooney, a coal miner's daughter from Pennsylvania, decided to take the amenities out to the diggings. Everybody cautioned her to stay in Dawson, but she bought a broken-down mule named Gerry and hauled the makings of the Magnet out to the Grand Forks. The Magnet drew and Belinda became rich.

There were lesser establishments. Mary's Hotel stood on the twentieth claim below Bonanza.
It offered coffee or pie for two bits, and in the summer she grew lettuce on the roof.

The action was downstream in Dawson. The Monte Carlo, one of the best-known spots for disportment, was the hangout of Little Ruby, an entertainer said to have the only pure-blooded American pimp on the Klondike. Of Ruby a discerning admirer purred, "She has the manners of a kitten and the morals of a cat."

Another twenty-four-hour night spot was the Opera House. Destroyed by fire, it reopened in 1899 on that grand old Canadian holiday, July 4th. The dominating figure, left-center, in wide-brimmed hat and wide-bowed mustache, is Arizona Charlie Meadows, authentic Indian fighter and barkeep.

The pride of Esther Duffy's establishment was not Irene (right) but the piano (center), the gift of an admirer. When Esther went broke she sold the piano for one thousand dollars to Babe Wallace, who hired Wilson Mizener (he claimed) to play it in a nightery called The Forks.

Hegg entitled this picture "Social Call on one of Dawson's Finest." He did not single out the one. Left to right are Black Prince, a prize fighter connected with the Monte Carlo; a man called Jack; Gertie Lovejoy, best known as Diamond Tooth Gertie; Cad Wilson, a baby-faced party girl who told one and all, "My mother said to be a good girl and pick nice clean friends—and I leave it to you, don't I pick 'em clean"; and Tommy Dolan, brother of comedian Eddie Dolan.

Dawson was struck by several fires that started in cabins occupied by ladies of ultimate accessibility. Eventually the authorities decreed that the most obvious of these entertainers must live on the outskirts. The area was called "Oshiwara" or "White Chapel" in honor of similar layouts in Tokyo and London. Hegg's notes indicate that he took this picture at midnight but do not explain the complete absence of clients on the boardwalks.

Americans outnumbered Canadians in Dawson more than seven to one. The Fourth of July was the major holiday of the year. Captain Jack Crawford, an alumnus of the Civil War, a veteran of the Indian fighting days in the West, and a partial graduate from illiteracy, was elected marshal of the 1899 parade. He recited a poem of his own manufacture which, in part, declared:

I love thee, Old Glory, with love
    that is true
And as pure as the stars in thy
    heavenly blue
There's no flag like my flag,
There's no flag like thine
Oh patriots, countrymen, comrades of mine.

Prominent among Captain Jack's countrymen was the U.S. Consul, who gave this dinner for the business community.

A feature of the New Year's Eve celebration in Pioneer Hall that year was a reading of the latest news of the Spanish-American War from a month-old issue of the Seattle Post-Intelligencer, just arrived by dog-team express from Skagway.

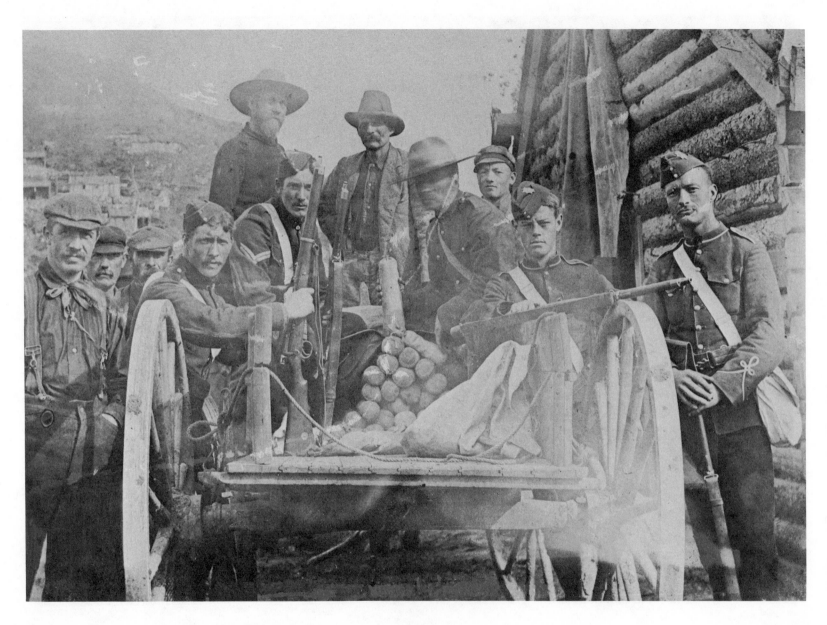

Robbery was rare on the Klondike, but Canadian troops guarded the movement of gold from the diggings to the river boats.

This shipment left Dawson on September 14, 1898, the last to go out that year. Its value was estimated at $1,500,000.

The Alaska Commercial Company store in Dawson had a ton and a half of gold waiting shipment after the winter of 1899–1900.

The Dark Sands of Nome

THE liberation of gold from the frozen muck of the Klondike tributaries was devolving from adventure to industry in the late fall of 1898 when the first rumors reached Dawson of a great new strike. Already there had been a score of minor stampedes out of Dawson to places of promise like Rampart City, where gold was found, and to Elk's Rump, which didn't exist.

Now the word was that great quantities of gold had been discovered by "three lucky Swedes" on Anvil Creek, a minor tributary of a meandering little river known as the Snake, which came into the Bering Sea a few miles south of a peninsula so obscure that it was said to have been named by a British draftsman who mistranslated a cartographer's query "?Name" as "Cape Nome."

In a town like Dawson, overpopulated by men disappointed in dreams of finding wealth at a stroke, but in the presence of walking transformations from poverty to richness, the rumor was enough to touch off a rush, though it took experience or foolhardiness for a man to start west with winter setting in. The first steamers up the Yukon the following summer, though, brought word that Nome had been worth the risk. Dawson veterans of experience and reputation for at least moderate truthfulness wrote of pan-outs averaging five dollars an hour. There was one report of three men taking eighteen hundred dollars a day from one claim. (Actually the whole Nome district yielded only eighteen hundred dollars the first season.)

The exodus was immediate. The American Consul at Dawson estimated that of eighteen thousand people in town when the steamer arrived, eight thousand started downstream the first week—a logistic impossibility, since boats were not available for that many. But certainly many who had not struck it rich on the Klondike saw a second chance gleaming on the western horizon, and left as soon as possible.

Hegg too. He was in Nome by August of 1899.

As few editorialists could resist remarking, there was no place like Nome. A year before, the beach had been just another stretch of bleakness with no more claim to world attention than a swath of the Sahara. A narrow shelf of dark sand rose from the sea to a line of bleached storm wrack; beyond, tundra humped into low, treeless hills. The distinguishing feature was a sluggish river that swerved across the soggy plain and, after a final turn that outlined a narrow spit, oozed into the sea.

Now Nome stretched along the spit, an improbable agglomeration of white tents and board buildings. The town that had taken root during the winter proliferated madly in the endless summer days of 1899. For four months the sound of hammering never ceased.

Nome was as strange for sourdoughs out of Dawson as for cheechakos fresh off the ships from Seattle. They might

recognize hundreds of faces, might know even the dogs, but all else was unfamiliar.

In the legendary but nonpervasive silence of the Yukon, the men had been accustomed to the whine of saws at the mills and the keening of steam whistles when some event necessitated the community's attention. But there were no forests on the Bering shore, and so no mills. Here the background sounds were of hammering, of waves slapping the beach, of gulls mewing as they wheeled overhead, and sometimes of gunshots—for claims were confused, tempers short, and the law far away. In Nome nobody tied down the mill whistle to announce a meeting—no mill; instead, when church bells rang on weekdays, the townsfolk assembled outside Tex Rickard's saloon.

There was no formal announcement of Nome's most improbable event—the discovery of gold in the very sands of the beach. The original strike was made on the Snake River. The early claims were along the creek. But sometime in the late spring of 1899 some fool—an unemployed reporter, some say; a scurvy-wracked sourdough waiting transportation Outside, according to others; a soldier named "Toughnut" Jack Clunin, by his own report—tried panning the beach sand, found color, dug down to a thin layer of reddish sand, swirled it in the pan, and was rewarded with the sparkle of countless grains of fine gold.

Here was the stuff of legend—gold from the sea. And

shipping companies, already feeling the pinch of the decline of the Klondike rush, spread the word. Nome, it was said, was the first convenient gold field. No mountains to climb, no plains to cross, just a pleasant cruise to a gold-flecked strand, then to hell with every boss.

It was true in a way. Except there was no port at Nome; the ships lay miles off the shallow beach, and the landing barges wallowed in only to wading distance. Sometimes passengers waited weeks to get ashore; many were left stranded without their baggage; others were carried back to St. Michael or Dutch Harbor. There was no sewage system in Nome. The public latrines—ten cents a visit—drained into the water supply. Bacilli spread typhoid, and mosquitoes spread malaria. Three boiled eggs cost a dollar and a thin steak (so tough, it was said, you couldn't stick your fork in the gravy), two dollars. And there wasn't beach enough, let alone gold enough, to go around.

When Hegg arrived, the beach was black with men and women elbowing for space in which to swirl pans and work rockers. There was no legal way to stake a claim on the tideflats. It was informally agreed that a man could work the sand within shovel-length of where he stood.

In Dawson, the Americans were foreigners, subject to laws they did not make. But the rules were clear and, it was generally agreed, fairly enforced. Nome was a chaos of democracy, a blizzard of community decisions based on little more than the pioneer tradition of self-government.

As a result there were two different plattings of the townsite, rival filings for nearly every claim, and when at last a federal judge arrived in July of 1900 he proved to be in league with a promoter who sought to jump the claims of all the best properties on Anvil Creek. Judge Arthur Noyes appointed his friend, Alexander McKenzie, as receiver for the mines with the right to sequester their entire production.

The mineowners obtained writs of supersedeas from the Circuit Court of Appeals in San Francisco. Judge Noyes calmly refused to honor them. McKenzie tried to withdraw the gold dust that was being held in a bank. The mineowners lined up in front of the vault and drove the receiver away at gunpoint.

After another trip to San Francisco, attorneys returned with two United States deputy marshals. They restored title to the original developers of the claim, returned their gold, and took McKenzie back to San Francisco, where he was jailed for contempt, the court holding that the shenanigans in Nome had "no parallel in the jurisprudence of this country." Judge Noyes himself was later found in contempt and fined.

A new judge, James Wickersham, arrived, and things settled down. Hegg's photos of Nome include a picture of the first grand jury, but no portraits of McKenzie or Noyes. He did make some excellent photographs of street scenes, particularly in winter when the days were short and the snows deep, and the saying was that "Even God left on the last boat." Another series shows one of the great storms which drove ships onto the beach and carried off houses.

His interest in process was as great as ever. He recorded the quick evolution of Nome mining from pan to rocker to dredge. No one was able to work a dredge successfully on the beach, but new deposits of gold were located inshore on land that in ages past had formed the beach. Rails were laid across the tundra, channels were dug, and great dredges were jockeyed into position. Then scoops ate at the hills and sluices washed the gravel.

Hegg's pictures of the process held true as long as gold was mined in Nome, which was for more than half a century. What had started as man against nature had become corporations against nature.

To say that they represented an end to his romanticism may be reading more into the photographs than Hegg felt. The bleakness of his shots of the sluices and dredges, the matter-of-fact quality of the pictures of the Wild Goose Railway may simply reflect the subarctic terrain and the often somber skies of the Bering littoral, rather than the sentiment of the man under the camera's cape. But there is a lyric quality to Hegg's shots of boats thrusting out through the breakers toward the waiting ships, and of the steamers moving south through the encroaching ice, that hints at a realization of an adventure ending.

It was easy to get almost to Nome, but the shallow beach and the heavy surf made landings hazardous.

Scows carried the prospectors in from ships lying several miles off the beach.

When the sea was calm the town expanded down the dark sands toward the ocean.

On the Fourth of July, when even the most gold-hungry paused
in their work, there wasn't enough room to go around.

Wyatt Earp owned "The Only Second Class Saloon in Alaska."

It was said that the bar at the post office was more crowded than that in any saloon, but only because it was closed half the time.

The first grand jury to meet at Nome considered indicting the judge.

It was discovered that the very sands of the beach were laced with gold.

Panning at tide's edge became a spectator sport.

Panning was too slow. Everybody tried to invent a machine which would separate the grains of gold from the ordinary beach sand.

Even the dance-hall girls found this type of rocking more rewarding.

Before long big machinery was brought in.

Dredges were hauled into position facing the old beach line back from the Bering.

Great hoses cut away the topsoil.

Gold-bearing dirt was washed along the riffled sluices.

Hillsides were dug out, washed down, piled up again.

The mining camp was institutionalized as industry.

Nome was swept each year by great storms rolling across the Bering Sea.

The sea flowed along the streets. Houses had to be tethered to bulkheads.

Not all could be saved. Annually buildings were swept out to sea.

Vessels anchored too close to shore ran the same risk. The Catherine Suddon *was caught in the surf and demolished on September 7, 1900.*

Three days later the Skookum was washed up on the dark sands of the Nome beach.

A year later the launch Evelyn *was pictured by* Hegg *as it came through the surf over the picked bones of the* Skookum.

The Siesta *and the* Teaser *were smashed in another storm.*

Sometimes it was too hot. Nome's first major fire came on May 25, 1901.

Sometimes too cold: Front Street in midwinter.

Sourdoughs said, "God left on the last boat."

*It took luck to guess which boat would be last. If the
freeze came early, the delay was half a year.*

The SS Senator lies off the ice pack.

Sometimes a crewman went ahead to find a path through the floes.

In one of his rare moments of humor, Hegg photographed one of the pleasures of winter in the far North: a sourdough picnic.

The Lost Legacy

AFTER Nome, Hegg went Outside. He married a woman who did not care for Alaska. But before long he was back. He visited the old places—Skagway, Lake Bennett, Dawson, Nome—but it was not the same. Mike Heney, the Irish Prince who had built the White Pass and Yukon Railway, was building the Copper River and Northwestern Railroad for the Guggenheims, and Hegg signed on as company photographer. Later he ran a studio in Cordova. Eventually Alaska came to seem wet and cold, and he went Outside for keeps, not rich, but without any regrets he felt worth mentioning.

Hegg went to Hawaii on assignment for a San Francisco newspaper and stayed for a year or so. He drifted back to Bellingham and opened another studio, this time at the corner of Elk and Holly. In 1953, at the age of eighty-six, he locked up a studio for the last time, wiped his eyes, and went to join a son in San Diego. He died in 1955.

Hegg's story was that of most of the hundred thousand persons who started north after the *Excelsior* and *Portland* brought out their pay loads. Pierre Berton, whose book *The Klondike Fever* is the most informative and entertaining story of the rush, estimates that fewer than half actually reached Dawson. Perhaps twenty thousand made any serious search for gold. About four thousand struck it rich. At least a dozen, perhaps as many as a hundred or more, stayed wealthy or comfortable for the rest of their lives.

Most would have done better, financially, if they had stayed home and worked for wages. But they had memories that set them apart, the Klondikers. Their annual reunions still radiate delight at the troubles they knew. The few who are left retain the mystique of a unique experience. They heard a call and answered, and ever since have felt themselves apart and privileged.

As the ranks of the sourdoughs thin and memories fade and distort, the legacy left by the journeyman Swede photographer, the quiet man who paid his way by photographing babies and weddings and dog teams but found time to be where important things were happening, became a mother lode for historians of the period. The legacy was nearly lost.

In his restless movements across Alaska, Hegg could not carry his files of glass negatives. He left caches behind him whenever he moved. Some he retrieved. Most of the plates he exposed at Nome were shipped Outside and stored in a house on Second Street in Seattle, where his wife stayed. When the marriage broke up, Mrs. Hegg left the files in the packing boxes. They were eventually acquired by the Seattle photographic firm of Webster and Stevens.

Another cache was left with Edward Larrs in Dawson. A Yukon flood washed into the studio and lapped at the wooden crates in which the plates were stored. The water haloed the edges of some but did no severe damage. When

Larrs closed his studio, he stored the plates between the inner and outer walls of the cabin and packed sawdust around them. He never returned.

Years later the secretary for a Dawson jeweler rented the cabin. While repairing an interior wall she reached through into the sawdust and cut her hand. Investigating, she pulled out a glass plate showing the Klondikers on Lake Bennett in 1898.

Here was a treasure. She had been longing for a greenhouse in which she could give flowers and vegetables a head start for the short Dawson growing season. She consulted her boss on how to get the gray stuff off the plates. He recognized them as valuable, bought a supply of greenhouse glass, and traded her even up.

Hegg's early negatives of the Bellingham Bay area also disappeared. They were simply missing when he came back from Alaska. Since no prints from them showed up on the commercial market, he always suspected that they actually had been used for a greenhouse on some Bellingham Bay stump ranch.

Hegg did keep a master file of prints from his negatives. These he mounted in forty-three big, old-fashioned, shoelace-bound albums. He had the albums with him when he came out of Alaska, but by the time he closed shop in Bellingham, they too were gone.

Individual prints from the Hegg negatives were becoming collector's items as the journalism of the rush became history. The most avid collector was a school teacher, Ethel Anderson Becker, the daughter of the man who had accompanied Hegg down the Yukon. She had gone over the pass herself as a child, and down the river, and had been photographed many times by Hegg as she played in the snow and mud of the golden city.

Now she set out to bring together all of Hegg's gold rush photos. Hegg approved of the project and gave her some pictures, but he told her he was sure that most were irretrievably lost. She kept trying. She asked J. W. Todd, Jr., the antiquarian who heads the Shorey Book Store in Seattle, to watch for Hegg photographs.

One day Lesley Melvin, an old Alaska hand living in Seattle, was strolling on Queen Anne Hill and saw a house being demolished. On the porch was a box partially buried under plaster. Melvin looked in the box and found 150 of Hegg's glass negatives. Todd obtained them for Mrs. Becker. He also arranged the purchase of the Nome pictures which had been acquired by Webster and Stevens.

That left the Dawson collection that had been stored in the cabin wall. Mrs. Becker tried several times to purchase them, but the owner wasn't interested in selling. She finally gave up. Years later, when she was living in Vancouver, B.C., a young couple called on her and said they had inherited some pictures of the gold rush. They had heard she was an expert. Were they worth anything? Thus she acquired the last of the glass negatives.

In the meantime Robert Monroe, the director of special collections for the University of Washington Library, had been gathering prints of Hegg photographs. In 1955 the Reverend Herbert Beatty on a visit to St. Vincent de Paul noticed a stack of large, brown photograph albums which, he was told, had been retrieved from a garbage truck. Here were thirty-three of the forty-three volumes in Hegg's master file. The minister brought them to Shorey's, and Todd bought them for the University of Washington. The other ten volumes have never been found.

In October, 1963, the University of Washington obtained Mrs. Becker's collection of plates and prints, bringing together most of Hegg's gold rush work known to be in existence. Bob Monroe has had prints made from all the negatives and copies from the master file where no negatives could be found. The entire collection has been cross-indexed, with the subject and date of the pictures recorded when such data are available.

Photographers at the turn of the century borrowed from each other with a casualness that is the dismay of a researcher. Most of Hegg's negatives carry his name in the corner. Some that he definitely took bear the studio imprint of Larrs and Duclos or of Webster and Stevens. Hegg, in turn, borrowed other men's work in some instances, but the only pictures reproduced here which are probably not Hegg's are those of Soapy Smith and Frank Reid.

Hegg's gold rush was one of the best. He saw Alaska and

the Yukon from a special point of view. He did not become rich, but he accumulated a treasure which Mrs. Becker, Mr. Monroe, Mr. Todd, and a scattering of sourdoughs and Alaska historians have saved for us.

List of Photographs